cook britain

by **Sainsbury's**

Over 120 delicious
sweet and savoury recipes

Welcome

This book celebrates the best of British food. With a bounty of fresh produce coming from our land and seas, it's no wonder we have such a rich food heritage and so many wonderful recipes in this country. As well as the classics, such as fish and chips, roast beef and, these days, chicken tikka masala, there's a treasure trove of delicious regional recipes just begging to be rediscovered. Join us on a tour of Britain with much-loved, traditional recipes from every region, and we'll let you in on some of the intriguing stories behind them.

We also look at how the calendar shapes our food and how the British spirit has shaped some of our more eccentric food traditions. And to help with your own celebrations, we've got irresistible ideas for street parties, picnics and afternoon tea.

There are clear, step-by-step instructions and each recipe has been tried, tested and tasted by Sainsbury's, so you can be sure of great results, whatever your level of cooking expertise. So, let's raise a toast to British food.
Happy cooking!

Fish & chips

Contents

Cranachan

Game pie

We've added these icons to make everything as clear as possible

 Recipes that can be on the table in 45 minutes or less

 Suitable for vegetarians

 Recipes containing 1 or more of your 5 a day. Aim to eat at least 5 different portions of fruit and vegetables a day. Fresh, frozen, dried, canned and juice all count

Traditional British cooking is often hearty, filling and full of flavour. Many of the fantastic recipes featured in this book were created when we led less sedentary lives, so our more calorific options should be enjoyed as part of a healthy balanced diet, with regular exercise.

Wash fruit, vegetables and herbs before use. Wash hands after handing raw meat or fish. Government guidelines recommend that adults consume no more than 6g salt a day. Sainsbury's encourages responsible drinking: visit drinkaware.co.uk

Best of

Great British recipes start with great British food, and Sainsbury's is proud to support our farmers and fishermen, who provide such fantastic-quality produce

Meaty matters

Many of our customers prefer to buy British meat and no wonder, as local farmers supply us with outstanding produce. Fresh ham, sausages and chicken at Sainsbury's is 100% British and we sell British lamb in season.
To prove our commitment to British farming, we aim to double the amount of British food we sell by 2020. British food has a great heritage, which we're proud to support. For example, our Taste the Difference dry-cure bacon is made to a family recipe dating back more than 100 years – each back of bacon is hand-rubbed with sea salt and sugar, cured for at least five days, then matured and air-dried for 14 to 20 days.

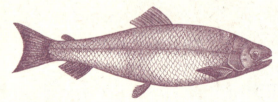

A good catch

We're the largest UK retailer of MSC-certified fish and seafood products, and all our fish carrying the Marine Steward Council ecolabel has been sourced in an environmentally responsible way. As well as encouraging sustainable fishing, we support the British fishermen who work hard to supply us with freshly caught fish from around the British Isles. Our Cornish sardines are caught within six miles of the Cornish coast from an MSC-certified fishery using local boats, and our British mackerel is hand-filleted and smoked by experts at a Plymouth smokehouse to give a fantastic rich flavour. All our fresh and smoked salmon is responsibly sourced from Freedom Food approved farms on the west coast and islands of Scotland, and we source freshly caught Scottish langoustines.

Top of the crops

Our commitment to providing great-tasting British products means offering them when they are in season and at their best. We offer more than 50 different varieties of home-grown British apples throughout the season and we support growers to introduce new varieties. We also sell more British pears than any other retailer. We work with local growers to make sure juicy British strawberries are on the shelves within hours of being picked and our summer sweetcorn is in store within 48 hours of being harvested. We use only British flour in our own-label sliced bread, made from wheat grown by a group of 300 farmers in East Anglia. Our customers like to support their local economy, so we plan to keep looking for the best regional products from local suppliers.

At Sainsbury's, we're aiming to double the amount of British food we sell by 2020

Cracking eggs

At Sainsbury's, we do not sell any eggs from caged hens, either boxed or as an ingredient in our own-brand products. We are the only retailer to offer high-welfare Woodland eggs in our core range. Hens love trees for shelter and protection, and our Woodland farms are planted with indigenous trees, which is good for welfare and biodiversity. We've also introduced regional eggs, supplied by local farms. This is good news all round. You're assured of where your eggs come from and how they were produced, 'food miles' – the distance from field to plate – are reduced and you're supporting the local economy. One such supplier is family-run Wood Farm, which provides eggs for Cambridgeshire. 'We have a genuine pride in our eggs,' says co-owner Charles Mear. 'We believe that shoppers today are more concerned about where food comes from and how it arrives on the supermarket shelf.'

Seasonal food diary

January Brussels sprouts, cauliflower, dates, duck, lemons, mackerel, pheasant, tuna

February Cod, oysters, parsnips, purple sprouting broccoli, rhubarb, sea bream

March Cucumbers, mussels, salmon, skate

April Crab, mint, new potatoes, parsley, pork, radishes, red mullet, sorrel, spinach

May Apricots, asparagus, coley, endive, gooseberries, lamb's lettuce, lobster, spring greens, spring lamb, spring onions, turbot

June Aubergines, blackcurrants, broad beans, cherries, fennel, globe artichokes, lettuce, marrows, new potatoes, plaice

July Basil, blueberries, garlic, greengages, peas, peaches, redcurrants, sole, Swiss chard, watercress, whitebait

August Celery, chicory, Chinese leaves, figs, gooseberries, grouse, haddock, hake, peppers, plums, pollock, samphire, sweetcorn, tomatoes, trout, venison

September Beetroot, blackberries, courgettes, damsons, guinea fowl, leeks, maincrop potatoes, megrim, raspberries, strawberries

October Autumn lamb, beef, Bramley apples, broccoli, celeriac, cranberries, dab, lemon sole, medlars, parsnips, pumpkins, salsify, turnips, wild duck

November Carrots, cavolo nero cabbage, clementines, kale, pears, quinces, rabbit, sardines, scallops

December Chestnuts, goose, halibut, herring, pike, swede, turkey

A potted history of British food

Once a bad joke, Britain's food is now regarded as among the best in the world. Here's an easy-to-digest guide to some of the landmarks of the past 500 years of British food

1869
Founded in 1869 by John James Sainsbury and his wife Mary Ann, Sainsbury's grows rapidly during the Victorian era. It becomes the largest grocery retailer in 1922, pioneering self-service retailing in the UK.

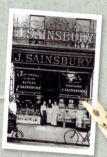

1850s
Today's three-course meal stems from the *Service à la Russe* introduced from Russia via France. Prior to this, all the dishes being served were on the table at the same time and diners helped themselves to whatever took their fancy.

1930
Sliced bread appears in Britain for the first time as commercial bread slicers are introduced in large bakeries. The slicing and wrapping of loaves is later banned during World War II as an economy measure.

1861
Mrs Beeton publishes her *Book of Household Management*. This guide to running a Victorian household contains more than 900 recipes and is the first book to include recipes printed in a format that is still used today.

1960s
With incomes starting to rise, Brits begin taking package holidays, bringing home inspiration for exotic new dishes such as spaghetti bolognese.

1940
Butter, sugar, meat, eggs, cheese, jam, tea and milk are rationed during World War II. People are encouraged to 'dig for victory' and plant vegetables to eat. Devising palatable recipes from ingredients such as powdered egg and Spam becomes a daily challenge.

1970s
In the decade that taste forgot, food goes space age. Convenience is king and all sorts of new products – including boil-in-the-bag dinners, Smash, the instant mashed potato, and Angel Delight, a powdered dessert – gain huge popularity.

Start here 👉

1500s The Tudor gentry enjoy lavish banquets prepared by large teams of kitchen and serving staff. Vast amounts of meat are consumed, but the rich tend not to eat vegetables, which they see as poor man's food. Imported sugar becomes increasingly popular, leading to extensive tooth decay among the wealthy.

1600s Britain goes coffee crazy, with more coffee shops opening up in London than you could imagine. Frequented by artists, intellectuals, merchants and bankers, the shops are a hive of political activity. Stockbrokers meet at Jonathan's Coffee House, in Change Alley, which eventually evolves into the London Stock Exchange.

1810 Bengali entrepreneur Sake Dean Mahomed opens Britain's first curry house in London's Portman Square, giving the Georgian gentry their first taste of spicy food. Ahead of his time, Mahomed goes bankrupt in 1812, but later opens the Indian Vapour Baths in Brighton and is duly appointed 'shampooing surgeon' to George IV and William IV.

CITY OF WESTMINSTER
SITE OF
HINDOOSTANE
COFFEE HOUSE
1810
LONDON'S FIRST
INDIAN RESTAURANT.
OWNED BY
SAKE DEAN MAHOMED
1759-1851
THE PORTMAN ESTATE

1847 The Vegetarian Society is formed against a backdrop of Victorian health reforms, with James Simpson (above) elected as its first president. By the 1880s, vegetarian restaurants are popular in London, offering cheap and nutritious meals.

1701 Jethro Tull invents the seed drill, which replaces hand-sowing and means that more grain can be harvested. Further advances herald the Agricultural Revolution, which transforms farming in Britain.

2000s The rise of the celebrity chef puts food in the spotlight. The 'Delia effect' occurs when shelves are emptied by shoppers in search of the cranberries Ms Smith recommends. Jamie sets about improving school dinners across Britain, Nigella is hailed as the domestic goddess, Gordon turns up the heat in *Hell's Kitchen*, while Hugh Fearnley-Whittingstall roots for 'real food'.

1980s The health-conscious 80s herald nouvelle cuisine – all style and very little substance. The microwave zaps its way into kitchens and jacket potatoes become hot news.

2012 Today, Britain has a well-deserved reputation for some of the finest foods, best chefs and most renowned restaurants in the world. There has been a huge resurgence of traditional foods and recipes, using locally produced, seasonal foods, so why not tuck in.

Classic British dishes

From the fry-up to the big family roast rounded off with an old-fashioned steamed pud, these are the dishes that spring to mind as 'British'. We may have our own versions, handed down through the generations, but all over Britain people are tucking into these time-honoured favourites and loving them. This is the food that puts the 'great' into British cooking

Savoury

Sweet

Full English breakfast

The 'full English' is known the world over, and Scotland, Wales and Northern Ireland have their own delicious variations of the fry-up

4 sausages
2 tomatoes, halved
1 x 300g pack Sainsbury's mini Portabella mushrooms
3 tbsp vegetable oil
8 rashers smoked back bacon
3 slices white bread, cut into triangles
4 slices black pudding
400g baked beans
4 eggs

Serves 4
Prep time: 5 mins
Cook time: 40 mins

Per serving
696 cals, **38.1g** fat, **9.8g** sat fat, **8.8g** total sugars, **2.5g** salt

1 Preheat the grill to medium-high. Preheat the oven to 120°C, fan 100°C, gas ½.

2 Grill the sausages for 15 minutes, turning occasionally, until golden and cooked through. Add the tomatoes, cut-side up, and the mushrooms for the last 10 minutes of cooking. Remove from the grill and keep warm in the oven.

3 Heat a large frying pan and add 1 tbsp oil. Add the bacon and fry until crisp and golden on both sides. Remove from the pan and keep warm.

4 Fry the bread in the pan for 2–3 minutes on each side, until golden. Add 1 tbsp oil to the pan, then fry the black pudding for 2–3 minutes, until crisp on both sides. Remove from the pan and keep warm.

5 Place the baked beans in a small saucepan and simmer for 5 minutes. Meanwhile, heat the remaining 1 tbsp oil in a clean, large frying pan, then crack in the eggs and fry until the white has just set and the yolks are still slightly runny.

6 To serve, divide between 4 plates. Great with mugs of tea.

Breakfast club

Ever-popular with hangover sufferers and holiday-makers, the 'fry-up' is one British classic that crosses the class divide – you'll find it in the swankiest of hotels as well as the greasiest of greasy spoons. The basic components include sausage, bacon, eggs, tomato and mushrooms. A full English sometimes also has black pudding, baked beans and fried bread, and a full Scottish might add tattie (potato) scones, haggis and oatcakes. An Ulster fry also features soda bread and potato farls (see recipes on pages 181 and 189), and the Welsh line-up is completed with laver bread (made from seaweed) and cockles.

Fish & chips
(with mushy peas)

If ever there was a British national dish, this has to be it. Loved from John O'Groats to Land's End, fish and chips is the perfect Friday night supper

1.35kg Maris Piper potatoes, peeled and cut into chips
2 tbsp olive oil
225g self-raising flour, plus extra for dusting
Pinch of salt
250-280ml lager, straight from the fridge
Sunflower oil, for deep frying
4 x 180g thick skinless and boneless cod or haddock fillets, from the fish counter
2 lemons, cut into wedges, to serve

For the mushy peas
500g frozen peas
6 mint leaves, chopped
4 tbsp half-fat crème fraîche

Serves 4
Prep time: 20 mins
Cook time: 40 mins

Per serving
902 cals, 24.5g fat, 4.9g sat fat, 7.2g total sugars, 1.1g salt

1 Preheat the oven to 200°C, fan 180°C, gas 6. Line a large baking tray with baking parchment.

2 Place the chips on the tray and toss with the olive oil. Season with salt and cook in the oven for 40 minutes, turning once, until crisp and golden.

3 Meanwhile, sift the flour and salt into a large bowl. Whisk in the lager until you have a smooth, lump-free batter with the consistency of double cream - it should be thick enough to coat the back of a wooden spoon.

4 Pour enough sunflower oil into a large, deep and heavy pan to come halfway up the sides. Heat over a medium heat until a cube of bread sizzles and crisps up within 30 seconds of being dropped into the oil.

5 Season the fish fillets with salt and freshly ground black pepper and dust lightly with flour. Dip 2 fillets into the batter, shaking off any excess. Using tongs, carefully lower the fillets into the hot oil and cook for 2-3 minutes on each side, until crisp, golden and cooked through. Drain on kitchen paper and keep warm. Repeat with the remaining 2 fillets.

6 Meanwhile, place the peas in a pan of boiling water and simmer for 2-3 minutes over a medium heat. Drain, reserving 2 tbsp cooking water. Stir the mint, crème fraîche and reserved water into the peas. Crush with a fork and season to taste with salt and freshly ground black pepper. Serve with the fish and chips, with lemon wedges on the side.

Top tip...
Adding ice-cold lager makes the batter light, crunchy and irresistible

A fisherman's tale...

In mid 19th-century Britain, the worlds of Irish immigrants – with their potato-dominated diet – and Jewish fried fish vendors collided and a national dish was born, spawning countless chippies on high streets and seaside piers up and down the land. About a quarter of all white fish and 10 per cent of the potatoes now sold in Britain are sold in fish and chip shops. Not to mention the pickled onions and eggs, curry sauce and mushy peas that go with them.

FISH & CHIPS

To drink...
An unoaked chardonnay is a great match for fish in creamy sauces

Fish pie

This is fantastic for family suppers, as everything comes to the table in one dish – fish, sauce, eggs and potatoes. Dig in!

430ml semi-skimmed milk
½ onion, sliced
4 peppercorns
1 bay leaf
800g Maris Piper potatoes, peeled and chopped
35g unsalted butter
3 medium eggs
25g plain flour
2 tbsp double cream
1 x 240g pack responsibly sourced Scottish salmon fillet, skinned and cut into 2–3cm cubes

200g smoked haddock, skinned and cut into 2–3cm cubes
200g white fish, such as pollock or cod, skinned and cut into 2–3cm cubes
1 tbsp chopped fresh flat-leaf parsley

Serves 6
Prep time: 15 mins
Cook time: 1 hour

Per serving
399 cals, 16.8g fat, 7.6g sat fat, 4.9g total sugars, 0.7g salt

1 Pour 400ml milk into a pan. Add the onion, peppercorns and bay leaf, and bring to the boil. Remove from the heat and leave to infuse for 15 minutes, then strain the milk into a jug, discarding the onion, peppercorns and bay leaf.

2 Meanwhile, place the potatoes in a pan of cold water. Bring to the boil, then simmer for 12–15 minutes, until tender. Drain and mash with the remaining 30ml milk and 10g butter. Season to taste with salt and freshly ground black pepper.

3 In the meantime, bring a small pan of water to the boil. Add the eggs and cook for 8 minutes, until just hard-boiled. Drain, then add cold water to the pan and leave until the eggs are cool enough to handle. Drain again, then remove the shells and cut the eggs into quarters.

4 Preheat the oven to 190ºC, fan 170ºC, gas 5. Melt the remaining 25g butter in a pan, then stir in the flour and cook for 1 minute. Remove from the heat and gradually add the infused milk, stirring well after each addition. Return to the heat and bring to the boil, stirring. Stir in the cream and season with salt and freshly ground black pepper.

5 Place the fish and eggs in a 1.5-litre ovenproof dish. Scatter over the parsley and pour over the white sauce. Spread a layer of mashed potato on top and fluff up with a fork. Cook the pie in the oven for 30–35 minutes, until the top is golden and the fish is cooked.

A dish to get hooked on

Fish pie is one of those dishes that has countless variations and, over the years, scores of chefs have claimed their recipe is the definitive one. While the origins of fish pie seem lost in the mists of time, there are some basic essentials. Bite-sized pieces of fish are smothered in a creamy sauce, then (like its cousins, shepherd's pie and cottage pie) the pie is topped with mashed potato - definitely not pastry. But that's where the agreement ends. Should a fish pie include boiled eggs or veg? Should the topping include grated cheese? And what about seafood, such as mussels or prawns? The only rule is, if it tastes good, do it! Jazz it up for a special occasion by adding more expensive fish. Add extra flavours, like chopped gherkin or capers, if you wish. The choice is yours.

Roast rib of beef

A rib of beef is the ultimate roast for a special occasion,
but a beef roasting joint will give you great results as well

4-rib joint of beef (ask at the
meat counter)
1 tsp plain flour
1 tsp English mustard powder
100ml port
1 tsp Dijon mustard
1 x 500g pouch Sainsbury's
Signature beef stock, heated

Serves 12
Prep time: 10 mins
Cook time: 1 hour, 35 mins
–2 hours depending on joint
weight, plus resting time

Per serving
585 cals, 39.8g fat, 20g sat
fat, 1g total sugars, 0.6g salt

1 Take the beef out of the fridge 2-3 hours before cooking to
allow it to come up to room temperature. Preheat the oven to
230°C, fan 210°C, gas 8. Weigh the beef to calculate the exact
cooking time – for medium rare, cook for 15 minutes per 450g
plus an extra 20 minutes; for well done, cook for 20 minutes
per 450g plus an extra 20 minutes.

2 Place the rib, fat-side up, in a roasting tin that holds it snugly.
Sift the flour and mustard together into a bowl, then dust it over
the fat using a tea strainer or fine sieve.

3 Roast the joint for 20 minutes, then reduce the oven temperature
to 200°C, fan 180°C, gas 6 and cook for the remaining cooking
time, basting the joint every 20–30 minutes.

4 Once the beef is cooked, take it out of the oven and transfer
to a serving platter. Loosely cover with foil and leave to rest for
20 minutes.

5 Meanwhile, skim any excess fat from the roasting tin. Place
the tin on the hob, add the port and cook gently for a few
minutes, scraping up any bits from the bottom, until reduced.
Stir in the mustard followed by the beef stock and simmer for
several minutes. Adjust the seasoning if necessary. Carve the
roast, adding any juices to the gravy. Great served with Yorkshire
puddings (see recipe on page 69).

To drink...
A good-quality
claret or rioja
will match the
richness of
the beef

Succulent meat with a mouthwatering crust — sheer perfection

Shepherd's pie

Traditionally a way of using up leftover roast meat, this can be made with diced or minced lamb – either way, it's a winner

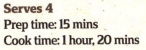

1kg Maris Piper potatoes, peeled and chopped
25g unsalted butter
1 tbsp olive oil
2 onions, finely chopped
2 carrots, peeled and finely chopped
2 sticks celery, finely chopped
2 cloves garlic, crushed
650g be good to yourself diced lamb
½ x 15g pack Sainsbury's fresh thyme, leaves picked
1 tbsp Worcestershire sauce
1 tsp cornflour, mixed with 1 tbsp cold water
500ml hot lamb stock

Serves 4
Prep time: 15 mins
Cook time: 1 hour, 20 mins

Per serving
500 cals, 13.2g fat, 6.1g sat fat, 10g total sugars, 0.2g salt

1 Preheat the oven to 180°C, fan 160°C, gas 4.

2 Place the potatoes in a pan of cold water. Bring to the boil, then simmer for 12-15 minutes, until tender. Drain and mash with the butter.

3 Meanwhile, heat the oil in a large saucepan over a medium heat and cook the onion, carrot and celery for 8 minutes. Add the garlic and cook for a further 2 minutes, until softened.

4 Stir in the lamb and cook for 10 minutes, until browned. Sprinkle over the thyme and stir through the Worcestershire sauce, cornflour mixture and lamb stock. Simmer gently for 20 minutes.

5 Transfer to a 22cm square baking dish, then spoon over the mash. Bake in the oven for 40 minutes, until golden and bubbling.

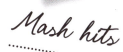

Mash hits

It was a piece of kitchen equipment that gave rise to the modern version of this meat-and-mash dish. In the 1870s, the new-fangled mincing machine made short work of processing offcuts of meat and a classic was born. It is widely believed that the dish came from the north of England and Scotland where there are large numbers of sheep. Shepherd's pie, as the name suggests, uses mutton or lamb, and is not to be confused with cottage pie, which contains minced beef. A regional variation is the Cumberland pie, which includes a layer of cheese and breadcrumbs on top of the mashed potato.

Sausages & mash
(with onion gravy)

One of those matches made in heaven, few things are more tempting to a hungry soul than a couple of bangers on top of a pile of fluffy, creamy mash

8 Cumberland sausages
1.2kg Maris Piper potatoes, peeled and quartered
30g unsalted butter
25ml semi-skimmed milk
400g petits pois

For the onion gravy

1 tbsp olive oil
3 onions, sliced
6 sprigs thyme
50ml red wine
1½ tbsp plain flour
1 tbsp redcurrant jelly
1 x 500g pouch Sainsbury's Signature beef stock, heated

Serves 4

Prep time: 15 mins
Cook time: 40 mins

Per serving

813 cals, 33.3g fat, 10.7g sat fat, 12.6g total sugars, trace salt

2 of 5 A-DAY

1 Preheat the oven to 190°C, fan 170°C, gas 5. Place the sausages on a baking tray and cook in the oven for 30–40 minutes, turning occasionally, until golden.

2 Meanwhile, place the potatoes in a pan of cold water. Bring to the boil, then simmer for 12–15 minutes, until tender. Drain and mash with the butter and milk. Season to taste with salt and freshly ground black pepper, then cover and set aside.

3 In the meantime, to make the gravy, heat the oil in a medium saucepan. Add the onions and thyme, and cook over a gentle heat for 30 minutes, until the onions are soft and just starting to caramelise.

4 Pour in the wine, bring to the boil and simmer for 1 minute. Stir in the flour and redcurrant jelly, then gradually add the stock and bring to the boil. Cook for 5 minutes, until slightly reduced, then season to taste with salt and freshly ground black pepper.

5 Meanwhile, cook the petits pois in a pan of boiling water for 2 minutes, then drain and serve with the sausages, mash and gravy.

To drink...
A hearty brown ale or stout will wash this down nicely

WAR-TIME
SAUSAGES
MADE IN SAINSBURY'S OWN MODEL KITCHENS
Grade A | PORK & PARIS 1'6
Meat Content not less than 70%
Government Maximum Price 1/6
Grade B | PORK 1'3
Meat Content not less than ... under 70%
Government Maximum Price 1/4

Banger boom

What's in a name? More to the point, what's in a sausage? In Victorian times, when the contents of a sausage were anyone's guess, they were referred to as 'little bags of mystery'. Later, after World War I, when meat was in short supply, they were padded out with cereal, water and other odds and ends. This made the sausages hiss and pop when they were cooked, leading some clever clogs to call them bangers. Today, the British banger is up there with the best, topping many a gastropub menu.

Steak & kidney pudding

Full of tender meat in a thick sauce, this classic steamed pudding – the ultimate comfort food – is guaranteed to hit the spot

200g light shredded vegetable suet
380g self-raising flour
½ tsp salt
Butter, for greasing
200g beef kidneys
700g braising steak, cut into 2cm dice
1 onion, sliced
3 tbsp plain flour
1 tbsp Worcestershire sauce
150ml beef stock

Serves 8
Prep time: 25 mins
Cook time: 4½ hours

....

Per serving
507 cals, 18.9g fat, 10.1g sat fat, 2.2g total sugars, 0.8g salt

1 To make the pastry, place the suet, self-raising flour and salt in a large bowl. Gradually add 250ml water, mixing until a soft dough is formed.

2 Tear off one-third of the dough and set aside. Roll out the remainder to a 30cm circle, about 5mm thick. Grease a 1.7-litre pudding basin with butter and line with the pastry circle, gently pushing into the sides of the basin. Using a sharp knife, trim any excess.

3 Skin the kidneys and cut in half. Using a pair of scissors, remove the sinews and discard. Cut the kidneys into small pieces, place in a large bowl with the steak and onion, and toss through the plain flour. Transfer the mixture to the pudding basin. Mix the Worcestershire sauce with the stock and pour over the meat.

4 Roll out the reserved pastry to form a lid large enough to fit neatly inside the basin. Place over the meat, then lightly dampen the edges of the lid with a little water. Fold over the pastry from the sides of the basin and press the edges together to seal.

5 Cover the pudding with a large disc of pleated baking parchment followed by a sheet of pleated foil (this allows the pastry to expand when cooking) and secure with kitchen string, trimming any excess foil.

6 Place on an inverted heatproof plate in a large saucepan and pour in enough boiling water to reach halfway up the sides of the basin. Cover and simmer for 4½ hours over a low heat, topping up with boiling water when necessary. Remove and cool a little before inverting onto a plate to serve.

Ooh, you are offal...

Surely one of Britain's national dishes, steak and kidney pudding has only been around since the mid-1800s. Beefsteak puddings had already featured on the British menu - indeed the poet and cook Eliza Acton's own creation, Ruth Pinch's Beefsteak Pudding, was named after one of the character's in *Martin Chuzzlewit* by Charles Dickens - but it wasn't until 1861 that the first recipe for the pud that we know and love today appeared in Mrs Beeton's *Book of Household Management*. Cockneys often refer to this national institution as Kate and Sidney pud.

To drink...

A lightly chilled glass of British ale will bring out the flavour of the gravy

Toad in the hole

Plump pork sausages, crispy Yorkshire pud and a rich onion gravy come together to make this family favourite

115g plain flour
¼ tsp salt
2 medium eggs, beaten, plus
1 egg white
180ml whole milk
8 good-quality pork sausages
2 tbsp sunflower oil
300g broccoli, cut into
medium-sized florets
400g petits pois

For the onion gravy
½ tbsp olive oil
1 onion, sliced
1 tbsp light brown soft sugar
2 tbsp plain flour

1 x 500g pouch Sainsbury's
Signature chicken stock, heated
1 tsp wholegrain mustard
2 sprigs fresh thyme, leaves picked
1 tsp Worcestershire sauce

Serves 4
Prep time: 20 mins
Cook time: 35 mins

Per serving
713 cals, 36.5g fat, 11g sat fat, 17.6g total sugars, trace salt

2 of 5 A-DAY

1 Preheat the oven to 220°C, fan 200°C, gas 7. Sift the flour and salt into a large bowl. Make a well in the centre and add the beaten eggs and egg white. Whisk them in, gradually drawing in the flour and adding just enough milk to make a paste. When all the flour is incorporated, whisk in the remaining milk until the batter is as thick as double cream. Set aside.

2 Place the sausages in a roasting tray and drizzle over the sunflower oil. Cook in the oven for 10 minutes, until the sausages are beginning to turn golden and the oil is very hot. Remove the tray from the oven and pour the batter mix around the sausages. Return to the oven and cook for 20-25 minutes, until the batter is risen and golden.

3 In the meantime, to make the gravy, heat the olive oil in a frying pan and fry the onion over a medium heat for 15 minutes, until soft. Stir in the sugar and cook for another 5 minutes. Stir in the flour, then gradually add the stock, stirring continuously. Bring to the boil and simmer gently for 5 minutes, adding the mustard, thyme and Worcestershire sauce for the last minute. Season to taste with salt and freshly ground black pepper.

4 Meanwhile, cook the broccoli in a pan of boiling water for 3-4 minutes, adding in the petits pois for the last minute. Drain and serve with the toad in the hole and gravy.

The hole truth

An everlasting favourite of British children, most of us know and love this dish as sausages (the toad) cooked in Yorkshire pudding batter (the hole). But it wasn't always so. In 1861, Mrs Beeton (pictured) described a version that used steak and kidney instead of sausages, and other early recipes called for cheap offcuts or leftovers of any kind of meat. *The Art of Cookery* (1747) even includes a recipe for 'pigeon in a hole'. Sausages became integral to toad in the hole during World War I – perhaps as a way to stop them exploding in the pan when frying – and the dish rapidly became a national hit.

Spotted dick

The perfect treat for a cold winter's day, this is a proper old-fashioned British pud that's long overdue for a comeback. A soft suet sponge studded with currants and flavoured with a hint of lemon zest, it's best when smothered with custard

On the spot

Schoolboy sniggers galore have led to this school dinners favourite being briefly renamed 'sultana sponge' and 'spotted Richard' on numerous occasions in the past decade. The earliest recipe for spotted dick appears in French chef and author Alexis Soyer's *The Modern Housewife* (1850), although similar dishes have been around for even longer. The 'spotted' part of the name clearly refers to the dried fruit, while the term dick could be derived from the word 'dough' or a contraction of 'puddink'. Traditionally, the dessert was boiled in cloth but is now usually baked or steamed. In more recent times, spotted dick has featured among the many classic British puds served at Hogwarts School of Witchcraft and Wizardry. Talk about magic...

250g self-raising flour
Pinch of salt
125g light shredded vegetable suet
80g caster sugar
Zest of 1 lemon
200g currants
150ml whole milk, plus
1-2 tbsp extra
Custard, to serve

Serves 8
Prep time: 15 mins
Cook time: 1½ hours
....
Per serving
552 cals, 24.8g fat, 15.1g sat
fat, 41.6g total sugars, 0.4g salt

V

1 Sift the flour and salt into a large bowl and stir in the suet. Mix in the sugar, lemon zest and currants.

2 Stir in enough milk to mix to a firm dough that feels moist. Gently knead for 1 minute, until the dough is firm enough to shape.

3 Shape into a fat roll about 20cm long, then place on a large rectangle of clingfilm. Wrap the clingfilm around the dough, twisting one end tightly, as if you were making a Christmas cracker. Leave the other end open to allow the dough to expand during cooking. Wrap the roll loosely in foil, sealing at each end.

4 Pour boiling water into a large lidded saucepan to a depth of 5cm. Fit a large steamer over the saucepan, pop the pudding in, cover and steam for 1½ hours, topping up with boiling water if necessary.

5 Remove from the steamer and leave to cool slightly before removing the foil and clingfilm. Slice and serve with custard.

Try this...
Add blackberries to your apple pie to give it some extra fruity flavour

Apple pie

Traditionally made with an upper crust only, this recipe uses Bramley apples for the perfect flavour and texture

250g self-raising flour, plus extra
for dusting
50g icing sugar, sifted
125g unsalted butter, cubed
1 large egg, beaten, plus extra for glazing
Splash of milk
4 large Bramley apples, peeled, cored
and chopped
1 tbsp cornflour
Zest and juice of 1 lemon
50g granulated sugar
½ tsp ground cinnamon
½ tsp ground ginger

Serves 4

**Prep time: 15 mins,
plus chilling time
Cook time: 40 mins**

Per serving
678 cals, 30.1g fat,
18.6g sat fat, 39.8g
total sugars, 0.6g salt

1 Place the flour, icing sugar and butter in a food processor and pulse until it resembles breadcrumbs. Add the egg and pulse until the dough comes together in a smooth ball, adding the milk if necessary. Wrap in clingfilm and chill in the fridge for 10-15 minutes.

2 Meanwhile, in a bowl, mix together the apples, cornflour, lemon zest and juice, sugar and spices. Place in a 1-litre ovenproof dish and brush the rim of the dish with a little beaten egg.

3 Preheat the oven to 190ºC, fan 170ºC, gas 5.

4 On a lightly floured surface, roll out the pastry to a thickness of 5mm. Place over the apple mixture and pinch the edges to secure onto the rim of the dish. Trim the edges. Make a 1cm hole in the centre of the pastry and decorate the top with leaves made from the leftover pastry, securing with beaten egg.

5 Brush the pastry with beaten egg and bake for 20 minutes. Reduce the oven temperature to 180ºC, fan 160ºC, gas 4, and cook for a further 15-20 minutes, until the crust is golden.

Sweet as pie

The earliest apple pies had an almost inedible pastry casing called a cofyn. Added to this, the costly and scarce nature of sugar in the 14th century meant that traditionally the pudding contained only fruits and spices. The first recipe was printed by the poet Geoffrey Chaucer, in 1381, and lists the ingredients as 'good apples, good spices, figs, raisins and pears'. Sugar was eventually introduced into the pudding by the 16th century. At this time, the dramatist and poet Robert Greene, in his prose *Arcadia*, was so fond of the dish he complimented a woman by saying, 'thy breath is like the steame of apple-pyes'.

Bread & butter pudding

Once just a humble pud that used up stale bread, this British classic now features on the menus of upmarket restaurants all over the country. Enjoy it served still wobbly and warm from the oven on a cold, wintry evening

Use your loaf

Born out of frugality and the need to use up stale bread, one of the earliest bread and butter puddings was recorded in 1723 in cook and author John Nott's *The Cooks and Confectioners Dictionary*. A childhood staple since Victorian times, the dish was originally known as 'white pot' due to the pale ingredients used – milk, butter and bread – with some reports citing the use of bone marrow instead of butter. White pots were sometimes made with rice instead of bread, which is thought to have marked the start of rice pudding in British cuisine.

40g unsalted butter, softened, plus extra for greasing
7 slices thick white bread, crusts removed
65g sultanas
400ml semi-skimmed milk
200ml double cream
3 medium eggs, beaten
50g caster sugar
Zest of 1 orange
2 tbsp demerara sugar

Serves 6
Prep time: 20 mins
Cook time: 35 mins

Per serving
453 cals, 26.4g fat, 15.1g sat fat, 28.8g total sugars, 0.5g salt

1 Preheat the oven to 180ºC, fan 160ºC, gas 4. Butter a 2-litre ovenproof dish.

2 Butter the bread, cut into triangles and arrange in the dish, pointing upwards. Scatter over the sultanas.

3 Whisk together the milk, cream, eggs, caster sugar and half the orange zest. Pour the mixture over the bread and set aside for at least 10 minutes.

4 Sprinkle the pudding with the demerara sugar and remaining orange zest, and bake in the oven for 30–35 minutes, until golden.

Jam roly-poly
(with homemade custard)

Another comforting pud for the colder months, this has a wonderfully soft texture, thanks to the vegetable suet

Butter, for greasing
320g self-raising flour, plus extra for dusting
80g caster sugar
150g light shredded vegetable suet
Pinch of salt
2 medium eggs, beaten
4 tbsp semi-skimmed milk
250g raspberry jam

For the custard
Yolks of 6 medium eggs
120g caster sugar
2 tsp cornflour
400ml whipping cream
400ml whole milk
1 vanilla pod, cut in half lengthways

Serves 8
Prep time: 25 mins
Cook time: 50 mins

Per serving
768 cals, 40g fat, 22.2g sat fat, 48.1g total sugars, 0.8g salt

1 Preheat the oven to 200°C, fan 180°C, gas 6. Butter one side of a sheet of baking parchment.

2 Sift the flour into a large bowl. Stir in the sugar, suet and salt. Add the egg and semi-skimmed milk and, using a wooden spoon, bring together to form a firm dough.

3 On a lightly floured surface, roll out the dough to a 30 x 20cm rectangle. Spread with the jam, leaving a 2cm border around the edge. Roll up tightly lengthways and pinch each end to seal.

4 Place on the greased side of the baking parchment and roll up. Wrap in a sheet of foil and bake in the oven for 45–50 minutes, until cooked through and light golden.

5 Meanwhile, to make the custard, whisk together the egg yolks, caster sugar and cornflour in a large bowl. Heat the whipping cream, milk and vanilla pod in a pan. When just about to simmer, remove from the heat and pour over the egg yolk mixture, whisking all the time. Remove the vanilla pod and discard. Pour the mixture back into the pan and place over a gentle heat for 5-10 minutes, stirring until the custard has thickened. Be careful not to boil. Slice the jam roly-poly and serve hot with the homemade custard.

Try this...
For a different flavour, make this roly-poly with apricot jam instead

Round and round

....

Called dead-man's arm in Victorian times, because in poorer homes it was often steamed and served in an old shirt-sleeve rather than a muslin cloth, jam roly-poly is most evocative of school dinners circa 1950. Mrs Beeton calls the suet-based dessert 'roly-poly jam pudding' in her *Book of Household Management* (1861). In Beatrix Potter's *The Roly-Poly Pudding* (1908), later republished as *The Tale of Samuel Whiskers*, Tom Kitten escapes the clutches of two rats planning to turn him into a roly-poly pudding.

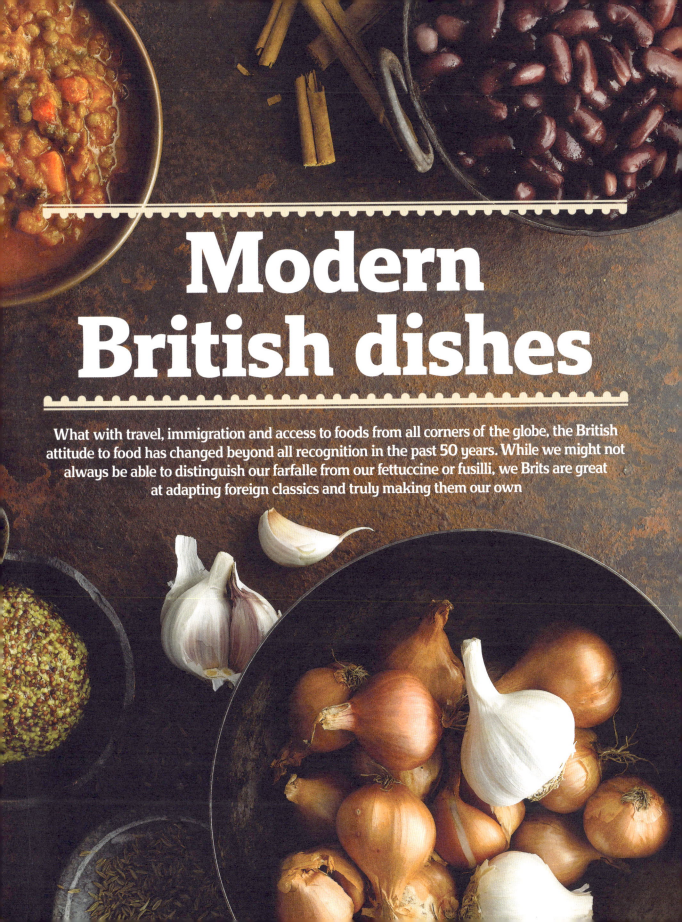

Modern British dishes

What with travel, immigration and access to foods from all corners of the globe, the British attitude to food has changed beyond all recognition in the past 50 years. While we might not always be able to distinguish our farfalle from our fettuccine or fusilli, we Brits are great at adapting foreign classics and truly making them our own

Chicken tikka masala

This creamy, delicately spiced curry was invented to satisfy the British appetite for meat with a hearty serving of gravy

4 skinless chicken breast fillets (about 500g)
½ tsp chilli powder
1 tbsp lemon juice
100ml natural yogurt
5cm fresh ginger, peeled and grated
4 tsp garam masala
2 tbsp vegetable oil
2 onions, thinly sliced
3 cloves garlic, finely chopped
1 tsp paprika
350g basmati rice
1 x 390g carton Sainsbury's chopped tomatoes
200ml hot chicken stock

3 tbsp double cream
1 x 28g pack Sainsbury's fresh coriander, chopped

Serves 4
Prep time: 20 mins, plus marinating time
Cook time: 30 mins

Per serving
690 cals, 15.7g fat, 5.3g sat fat, 10.8g total sugars, 0.6g salt

1 Cut the chicken into medium-sized pieces and place in a bowl. Add the chilli powder, lemon juice, yogurt, half the ginger and 1 tsp garam masala, and mix well. Cover and place in the fridge for at least 1 hour, or overnight.

2 If using wooden skewers, soak them in water for at least 30 minutes before cooking. Preheat the grill to high. Thread the chicken onto the skewers and place on a baking tray. Grill for 5 minutes on each side, until lightly browned and cooked through so no pink remains. Remove the meat from the skewers.

3 Meanwhile, heat the oil in a large pan and fry the onions over a medium heat for 10 minutes, until golden. Stir in the garlic and remaining ginger, and cook for 1 further minute. Stir in the paprika and remaining 3 tsp garam masala, and fry for about 1 minute, until the spices release their aromas. In the meantime, cook the rice following pack instructions.

4 Pour in the tomatoes and stock, and bring to the boil. Turn down to a low-medium heat and simmer for 5 minutes, until slightly thickened. Stir in the cream and add the chicken pieces. Simmer for 1 further minute, then stir through half the coriander.

5 Garnish the chicken tikka masala with the remaining coriander and serve with the rice. Great served with warm naan bread.

Curry flavour

As Indian as haggis, whisky and shortbread, chicken tikka masala is believed to have been created in a Glasgow curry house. A customer thought the tandoori chicken was too dry and asked for sauce to go with it, so the chef created a creamy yogurt and spice accompaniment. In 2001, foreign secretary Robin Cook called it a 'true British national dish' because it reflects how the country absorbs and adapts external influences. We love chicken tikka masala so much that hotels in Bombay have now put it on their menus to satisfy the demands of British tourists.

Sweet & sour chicken

The sweetness of the pineapple and the piquant flavours of the sauce create a mouthwatering dish that's been a takeaway favourite for decades

100g self-raising flour
175ml soda water, chilled
Vegetable oil, for frying
500g chicken breast fillets, chopped
into 2.5cm pieces
2½ tbsp cornflour
1 tbsp groundnut oil
1 red pepper, deseeded and chopped
1 green pepper, deseeded and chopped
2 cloves garlic, finely chopped
4cm fresh ginger, peeled and
finely chopped
2 red chillies, deseeded and
finely chopped, plus 1 sliced red chilli
to garnish
1 x 432g tin Sainsbury's pineapple
pieces in natural juice, drained and
juices reserved
1 tbsp tomato ketchup
3 tbsp light soy sauce
3 tbsp dry sherry or rice wine
1 tbsp light brown soft sugar
1 x 225g tin water chestnuts
in water, drained
350g basmati rice
4 spring onions, sliced, to garnish

Serves 6
Prep time: 20 mins
Cook time: 30 mins

Per serving
580 cals, 12.4g fat, 1.8g sat fat,
14.9g total sugars, 1.4g salt

1 Preheat the oven to 120°C, fan 100°C, gas ½. To make a batter, place the flour and soda water in a large bowl and whisk together until lump-free. Pour enough vegetable oil into a large saucepan to reach a quarter of the way up. Heat until a small cube of bread browns in 30 seconds when added to the pan. Dust the chicken in 1 tbsp cornflour, then dip in the batter and shake off the excess. Fry in batches for 4 minutes, until golden and cooked through so no pink remains. Drain on kitchen paper, then keep warm in the oven.

2 To make the sweet and sour sauce, heat a large frying pan over a high heat and add the groundnut oil. Add the peppers and fry for 2-3 minutes. Add the garlic, ginger and finely chopped chillies, and fry for another minute.

3 Mix the remaining 1½ tbsp cornflour with 3 tbsp reserved pineapple juice and add to the pan along with 350ml water. Add the pineapple pieces, ketchup, soy sauce, sherry, sugar and water chestnuts. Bring to the boil, then simmer for 8 minutes.

4 Meanwhile, cook the rice following pack instructions. Serve with the chicken, topped with the sweet and sour sauce. Garnish with the sliced red chilli and spring onions.

To drink...
Aromatic whites like gewürztraminer work best with this fruity dish

Take it away

Sweet and sour is more than likely the first dish that springs to mind whenever we think of Chinese food. It became popular in Britain after World War II, when servicemen returned from the Far East with a new taste for oriental cuisine. In the 1960s, thousands of people came to Britain from Hong Kong, with a number of entrepreneurial newcomers opening restaurants and takeaways. Our love affair with Chinese food has continued ever since.

Spaghetti bolognese

'Spag bol' may not be a strictly authentic Italian recipe, but it's delicious and easy, and Britain just can't get enough of it

1 tbsp olive oil

4 rashers smoked streaky bacon, chopped

1 carrot, peeled and coarsely grated

2 sticks celery, finely chopped

1 onion, chopped

2 cloves garlic, crushed

1 x 500g pack Sainsbury's lean beef steak mince

100ml red wine

150g mushrooms, finely chopped

1 x 390g carton Sainsbury's chopped tomatoes

1 tsp Sainsbury's Italian herb seasoning

2 tbsp tomato purée

250ml hot beef stock

¼ x 28g pack Sainsbury's fresh basil, shredded

400g spaghetti

Freshly grated parmesan, to serve

Serves 4

Prep time: 20 mins

Cook time: 1 hour

Per serving

772 cals, 27.4g fat, 11.6g sat fat, 12.3g total sugars, 1.3g salt

1 Heat the oil in a large lidded pan, then add the bacon and fry over a medium heat for about 3 minutes, until golden. Add the carrot, celery, onion and garlic, and cook for a further 10 minutes, until beginning to soften.

2 Add the mince and cook until browned, breaking up the meat with a wooden spoon.

3 Pour in the wine and cook until it has reduced by a third. Add the mushrooms, tomatoes, herb seasoning, tomato purée and stock, then reduce the heat. Cover and simmer for 30-40 minutes, until rich and thick. Stir in the basil and season to taste with salt and freshly ground black pepper. If the mixture is a little thin, leave the lid off for the last 10 minutes.

4 Meanwhile, cook the spaghetti following pack instructions, then drain and return to the pan. Stir the bolognese into the pasta and serve sprinkled with parmesan.

To drink... An Italian red like chianti or valpolicella will match this rich sauce

Not quite like mamma made...

For many people growing up in post-war Britain, spaghetti bolognese was their first taste of 'foreign' food, but pairing bolognese sauce with spaghetti is not the done thing in its birthplace – the northern Italian city of Bologna. Since spaghetti itself hails from further south, the locals prefer to serve their sauce with larger pasta shapes, such as tagliatelle or lasagne. The popularity of bolognese sauce is thought to have been spread around the UK and the US by soldiers returning home from Italy after World War II. Spaghetti was the most available pasta shape, so 'spag bol' was born.

Thai green chicken curry

The spices and chilli in this easy-to-make Thai favourite are delicately balanced to create a beautifully fragrant curry

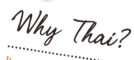

1 tbsp vegetable oil
3 tbsp Thai green curry paste
1 tbsp dark brown soft sugar
1 x 500g pack Sainsbury's chicken breast fillets, cut into chunks
1 tbsp dried kaffir lime leaves (or zest of 1 lime, if unavailable)
1 x 400ml tin coconut milk
1 tsp fish sauce
2 lemongrass stalks, bashed
150g frozen peas
1 x 200g pack Sainsbury's trimmed mange tout
250g jasmine rice
½ x 28g pack Sainsbury's fresh coriander, roughly chopped, plus extra to garnish
Juice of 1 lime, plus lime wedges to serve

Serves 4
Prep time: 10 mins
Cook time: 35 mins

Per serving
593 cals, 16.1g fat, 10.4g sat fat, 8.6g total sugars, 0.6g salt

1 Heat the oil in a large frying pan. Add the green curry paste and sugar, and fry over a medium-high heat for 1 minute.

2 Add the chicken pieces to the pan and fry for 5-10 minutes, until browned all over. Stir in the kaffir lime leaves or lime zest, coconut milk, fish sauce and lemongrass, and bring to a gentle simmer. Cook for 20 minutes, until thickened slightly, then add the peas and mange tout and cook for a further 2-3 minutes. Meanwhile, cook the rice following pack instructions.

3 Remove the lemongrass from the curry and discard, then stir through the coriander and lime juice. Serve with the jasmine rice, sprinkled with coriander, with lime wedges on the side.

Why Thai?

It wasn't too long ago that lemongrass, kaffir lime leaves and coconut milk would have been almost impossible to find in the UK, but these days they're pretty much standard fare. Thai food really started to catch on in Britain during the 80s, as more and more of us went on holiday to Thailand. Top of the menu has to be Thai curry. Fresh and aromatic, it can now be found in most pubs and usually comes in red and green variations, depending on the colour of the chillies used. Unless you're a true devotee, there's no shame in using a ready-prepared curry paste.

Chilli con carne

Both Texas and Mexico lay claim to the origins of this spicy, meaty dish, but with a few tweaks over the years, it's become a hot favourite in Britain, too

A spicy story

Chilli con carne is one dish we've really taken to our hearts, to the point of serving it Brit-style, bursting out of a baked potato. But our version is quite different from the real deal, the origins of which are hotly disputed. Popular theory has it that chilli con carne is from Mexico, but the dish probably comes from America's southwest and originally consisted of chopped or ground beef, garlic, chillies, onions and cumin. In the 1880s, it was prepared in cauldrons over campfires in downtown San Antonio by colourfully dressed Mexican women known as 'chilli queens', who sold it by the bowl. Passers-by would be drawn in by the potent aromas and the mariachi musicians who would serenade diners. Known as a 'bowl of red', chilli con carne became the official dish of Texas in 1977.

1 tbsp vegetable oil
2 onions, chopped
2 cloves garlic, chopped
1 x 500g pack Sainsbury's lean
beef steak mince
1 tbsp plain flour
3 tbsp tomato purée
300ml hot beef stock
1 x 390g carton Sainsbury's
chopped tomatoes
1 tsp hot chilli powder
1 tsp dried oregano
1 large green pepper, deseeded
and diced
1 x 410g tin Sainsbury's red kidney
beans in water, drained and rinsed
240g basmati rice
Lime wedges, to serve

Serves 4
Prep time: 15 mins
Cook time: 50 mins
....

Per serving
650 cals, 20.7g fat, 8g sat fat,
8.1g total sugars, 0.3g salt

1 Heat the oil in a large, deep lidded pan. Add the onions and garlic, and cook for about 5 minutes. Add the mince and cook for 2 minutes, stirring well.

2 Sprinkle over the flour and stir in. Add the tomato purée, beef stock, tomatoes, chilli powder and oregano.

3 Bring to the boil, stirring, then reduce the heat to a simmer. Cover and cook gently for 30 minutes.

4 Add the green pepper and kidney beans. Cover again and cook for a further 10 minutes, then season to taste with salt and freshly ground black pepper. Meanwhile, cook the rice following pack instructions. Serve the chilli with the rice and a wedge of lime. Great with tortilla chips.

Burger

Originally from Germany, this all-American classic has become a sure-fire winner all over the world

1 x 500g pack Sainsbury's lean
steak mince
1 red onion, finely chopped
1 tbsp English mustard
25g fresh breadcrumbs
1 tbsp finely chopped fresh
flat-leaf parsley
1 medium egg, beaten
1 tbsp olive oil
4 slices Cheddar (about 80g)

For the accompaniments
4 Sainsbury's sesame seed rolls,
halved
4 leaves from 1 round lettuce
2 tomatoes, sliced
2 gherkins, sliced
3 tbsp tomato ketchup

Serves 4
**Prep time: 15 mins,
plus chilling time
Cook time: 15 mins**

....

Per serving
**567 cals, 28.4g fat, 12.5g sat fat,
9.6g total sugars, 1.7g salt**

1 Place the mince, onion, mustard, breadcrumbs, parsley and egg in a large bowl and mix together. Season to taste with salt and freshly ground black pepper. Divide the mixture into 4 balls, then flatten into patties. Place on a plate, cover with clingfilm and chill in the fridge for 1 hour to firm up.

2 Preheat the grill or barbecue. Rub a little oil over the burgers and cook them over a medium heat for 6-7 minutes on each side, until cooked through. (Alternatively, you could cook the burgers in a preheated oven at 180°C, fan 160°C, gas 4 for 15-20 minutes.) Pop a slice of cheese on top of each burger for the last 30 seconds.

3 Meanwhile, griddle the rolls on the cut sides. Place a lettuce leaf on the bottom half of each burger bun. Top each with tomato slices and a cooked burger. Place a few gherkin slices on top of each burger, along with a dollop of ketchup. Pop on the top halves of the buns and serve at once.

To drink...
A light and refreshing lager would be a great match for this burger

Bun voyage!

Ground meat has been shaped into patties all over the world for centuries, but the 'hamburger' didn't appear until the late 19th century, when Germans emigrating to the US from the port city of Hamburg took the dish with them. The now ubiquitous burger is eaten across the globe, thanks to the fast food explosion that has taken place in recent years. Undisputed burger connoisseurs, Americans consume more than 14 billion of them annually. Hold those fries!

Pavlova

Australians and New Zealanders can bicker for as long as they want over the origins of this dreamy, creamy dessert. Brits, in the meantime, will be tucking in

Aussie rules?

Named after the famed Russian ballerina Anna Pavlova (pictured) – the dessert is supposed to represent her tutu – the origin of this most delectable meringue creation is the cause of fiery debate between Australia and New Zealand, with each country claiming it as their own. In the meantime, in Britain, we've been happy to adopt pavlova ourselves, often swapping the original passionfruit topping for local fruits such as rhubarb, raspberries and blackberries. But those Kiwis aren't giving it up without a fight. In 1999, they created a giant 45-metre long monster, dubbed 'Pavzilla', to prove their pavlova supremacy.

4 medium egg whites
225g caster sugar
2 tsp cornflour, sifted
1 tsp white vinegar
200ml whipped cream
500g seasonal fresh fruit
1 tsp icing sugar

Serves 6
Prep time: 20 mins,
plus cooling time
Cook time: 1 hour

Per serving
337 cals, 13.6g fat,
8.4g sat fat, 46.3g
total sugars, 0.1g salt

1 Preheat the oven to 150ºC, fan 130ºC, gas 2.

2 In a large bowl, whisk the egg whites until stiff peaks form, then gradually add the sugar, beating until smooth and shiny. Fold in the cornflour and vinegar.

3 Spoon the mixture onto a baking tray lined with baking parchment. Using a palette knife, shape into a 25cm circle and make a slight dip in the middle.

4 Place in the oven and reduce the temperature to 120ºC, fan 100ºC, gas ½. Cook for 1 hour, then turn off the heat and leave the meringue to cool in the oven for 3-4 hours.

5 Once cool, whip the cream until soft peaks form, then fill the meringue. Top with the fruit and sprinkle over the icing sugar.

For added decadence, serve with a dessert wine, such as sauternes

Chocolate mousse

We have the French to thank for this light and fluffy dessert, an out-and-out classic for chocolate lovers across the nation

1 x 200g bar Sainsbury's Belgian dark cooking chocolate, broken up
6 medium eggs, separated
3 tbsp caster sugar
1 tbsp Tia Maria (optional)
1 x 150ml pot Sainsbury's double cream, softly whipped

Makes 6
Prep time: 20 mins, plus chilling time
Cook time: 5 mins

Per serving
411 cals, 29.1g fat, 16g sat fat, 27.1g total sugars, 0.2g salt

1 Melt all but 2 chunks of the chocolate in a heatproof bowl over a pan of gently simmering water, taking care not to let the bowl touch the water, then remove from the heat and leave to cool for 5 minutes.

2 Meanwhile, place the egg yolks and sugar in a medium-sized bowl and whisk with an electric hand mixer until pale and thickened. Stir in the melted chocolate and Tia Maria, if using, and set aside.

3 In a separate bowl, whisk the egg whites with an electric hand mixer until stiff. Add a large spoonful to the chocolate mix and carefully fold in using a large metal spoon, then gently fold in the remaining egg whites. Try not to over-mix or the texture of the mousse will be heavy.

4 Spoon into 6 cups or dessert glasses, add a dollop of whipped cream and grate the remaining 2 chunks of chocolate over the top. Chill in the fridge for 2 hours before serving.

Cook's note: this recipe contains raw eggs

Fluff it up

A favourite standby of 60s British dinner parties, mousse, which means 'foam', originated in France in the 18th century. Earlier recipes yielded more of a chocolate pudding-type dish than the light and airy mousse we know and love today. It was the introduction of electric mixers that made the process of whipping egg whites much more effective, creating a fluffier mousse. A new sensation came in 1977, when a chef in New York created a white chocolate version – until this point it was always made with dark chocolate. It wasn't long, however, before the original mousse regained top spot on the menu.

Cheesecake

The cheesecake dates back to Ancient Greece and is now found in all shapes and sizes around the world. Try our delicious cherry-topped, no-bake version ...

On your marks, get set, cheesecake

Cheesecake is thought to have originated in Ancient Greece – in fact, legend has it that it was served to athletes during the first Olympic Games held in 776 BC, as part of a diet that consisted mainly of cheese, namely feta. The Romans, who were great cheesemakers, made the dessert their own and spread it throughout Europe.

Eastern European immigrants were probably responsible for later taking the cheesecake to the US, where it soared to new heights of popularity. New Yorkers put their own spin on it and the famously smooth-tasting New York-style cheesecake was born. Different countries have their own cherished variations, often using different cheeses. Some are topped with fruit, toffee, nuts or chocolate, while others are served simply as they come. Some are baked, while others are chilled. And some are sweet, while others are savoury. The cheesecake really is a multicultural dish.

200g digestive biscuits
75g unsalted butter, melted
2 x 200g packs Sainsbury's
soft cheese
150g caster sugar
200ml double cream
200g white chocolate, melted

For the topping
400g fresh cherries, pitted
50g golden caster sugar

Serves 12
Prep time: 20 mins
Chilling time: 4 hours
....

462 cals, 30g fat,
18.7g sat fat, 35.2g
total sugars, 0.5g salt

1 Line a 25cm springform tin with clingfilm. Crush the digestive biscuits in a bowl and pour the melted butter over the top. Mix together, then spread over the base of the tin, pressing down firmly. Place in the fridge to set.

2 In a large bowl, beat the soft cheese with the caster sugar until well combined. In a medium bowl, whip the double cream until it forms soft peaks. Add the melted chocolate and whipped cream to the cream cheese mixture and fold through. Pour into the tin and leave to set in the fridge for 4 hours.

3 Meanwhile, in a large frying pan cook the cherries over a medium heat, until beginning to soften. Sprinkle over the sugar and simmer until the sugar becomes syrupy and coats the cherries. Leave to cool.

4 When ready to serve, gently release the cheesecake from the mould, remove the clingfilm and place on a serving plate. Top with the cherries, drizzle with the syrup and cut into slices.

Food tour of britain

Each region of Britain enjoys a unique natural larder and traditional recipes cherished by generations of locals. Join us on a tour to discover the best food and drink from every corner of the land, and find out about regional specialities and some of the fascinating stories behind the food

Scotland

Northern Ireland

The North

The Midlands

East Anglia

Wales

The Southeast

The Southwest

The best of
the North

The North

Yorkshire Dales

The North

With its tranquil valleys, untamed fells and clear coastal waters, northern England is blessed with an abundance of great foods, and there are plenty of traditional local recipes to take advantage of the produce

The north of England is an area rich in history and culinary treasures. The distinct counties of this vast region are full of character with a great food heritage to boot. Referred to by proud locals as 'God's own county', Yorkshire is England's largest county. Its varied landscape – wild moors, rolling dales, old market towns and rugged coastline – produces delicious local food. Cattle and sheep graze on the rich pastures and a variety of crops thrive here. Also in the northeast there's Northumberland, with its rich arable land and famous oysters farmed off the Holy Island of Lindisfarne.

Over on the west side there's Lancashire, which also produces a fantastic natural harvest. Brown shrimps are fished from Morecambe Bay's shallow waters and Lancashire cheese is made from local milk to traditional methods. Further up there's Cumbria, the place to go for Kendal mint cake and the Cumberland sausage.

As you'd expect from a place with ideal terrain for rearing sheep, cattle and pigs, meat features heavily in many traditional Northern dishes. From hearty stews like Scouse to Cumberland sausages and black pudding, the hero recipes of the North make use of what was readily available and economical back in the day. In fact, this traditional no-frills fare of meat and two veg, with a little seafood here and there, has enjoyed a revival in recent years, with top chefs whipping up modern interpretations in some of our best restaurants. No matter what the stories are behind the food, we can credit the North for giving us proper pub grub, slow-cooked with love.

In the pink

It took Janet Oldroyd Hulme (pictured), of E Oldroyd & Son in Leeds, six years to gain top level Protected Designation of Origin (PDO) status for her rhubarb. Yes, that's right, Yorkshire forced rhubarb has been awarded Protected Designation of Origin (PDO) status, alongside Stilton, Jersey Royal potatoes and Cornish clotted cream, meaning that only rhubarb produced in an area of nine square miles – the rhubarb triangle – can carry the name of Yorkshire forced rhubarb. There are 11 growers in the triangle, located between Rothwell, Wakefield and Morley. Among them are the Oldroyds, who have been in the business for more than a century and are the main supplier of rhubarb to Sainsbury's. The PDO status has alerted shoppers to how good Yorkshire forced rhubarb is, says Janet. 'People certainly look for it. It has a better flavour and is more tender than outdoor-grown rhubarb.'

5 foods the area is famous for

Black pudding This blend of pig's blood, oatmeal and onions is often enjoyed in a full English breakfast. It tastes better than it sounds.

Rhubarb Yorkshire's so well known for these prized pink sticks that it has its own 'rhubarb triangle'.

Brown shrimps These tiny crustaceans from Morecambe Bay are traditionally cooked in butter and spices before being sealed to make potted shrimp.

Wensleydale cheese The original recipe for this crumbly cheese was passed down by monks in 1150 and has been enjoyed ever since – especially by cheese connoisseur Wallace of Wallace and Gromit fame.

Yorkshire pudding This simple batter pudding has become one of Britain's most famous dishes.

Did you know? The historic fishing port of Whitby provided the atmospheric backdrop for Bram Stoker's famous gothic novel, *Dracula*. Shipwrecked off the Yorkshire coast, the bloodthirsty vampire Count Dracula comes ashore to prey upon the people of Whitby. Rest assured that today human blood is strictly off the menu, but you might want to buy some garlic just in case…

Liquorice Pontefract cakes

Thanks to its deep sandy soil, Pontefract in Wakefield is at the heart of the UK's liquorice industry. The herbaceous root was used as a medicine until Pontefract's famous 'Yorkshire Penny' cake turned it into a sweet. Liquorice is such a key part of Pontefract's heritage that the locals celebrate it every year at the Pontefract Liquorice Festival. It takes Allsorts.

To serve...
Great with crusty white bread, pickled red cabbage and pickled onions

Scouse

Make this hearty lamb and vegetable stew for your family and you'll be sharing in the culinary history of our seafaring nation

2 tbsp olive oil
800g lamb neck fillet, cut into 3cm cubes
1 onion, roughly chopped
2 sticks celery, roughly chopped
3 carrots, peeled and roughly chopped
2 leeks, roughly chopped
2 tbsp plain flour
1 litre hot lamb or chicken stock
1 bouquet garni (2 bay leaves and a small bunch of thyme and flat-leaf parsley tied together with string)
2 medium Maris Piper potatoes, peeled and cut into large chunks

Serves 8
Prep time: 20 mins
Cook time: 1 hour, 10 mins

Per serving
324 cals, 17.5g fat, 7g sat fat, 4.6g total sugars, trace salt

1 Heat the oil in a large flameproof casserole dish over a high heat. Season the lamb with salt and freshly ground black pepper and fry, in batches, until golden all over. Remove the lamb and set aside.

2 Add the onion, celery, carrots and leeks to the pan and sauté for 3–4 minutes. Add a splash of water to help the vegetables steam, then cover with a lid and cook for another 3 minutes. Sprinkle in the flour and stir well.

3 Return the lamb to the pan. Add the stock and bouquet garni, then bring to the boil before covering and simmering for 30 minutes. Add the potatoes, then simmer uncovered for a further 15 minutes, until the lamb and potatoes are tender and the sauce has reduced a little. Remove the bouquet garni, season with salt and freshly ground black pepper and serve.

Stew ahoy

When we hear the word 'scouse' we think of all things Liverpudlian, but this slang term didn't originate in Merseyside – it comes from *lapskaus*, the Norwegian word for stew. In the 18th and 19th centuries the major port of Liverpool was inundated with foreign sailors, many from Norway. Their staple meal, and that of most working-class folk, was a 'pan of scouse' consisting of a cheap cut of lamb with onions, carrots and potatoes simmering away on the stove, served with pickled cabbage and bread to mop up the juices. As a Liverpudlian saying goes, scouse should be firm enough 'for a mouse to trot over it'.

Pease pudding
(with gammon)

One of Britain's oldest and most traditional dishes, this comforting pea stew goes perfectly with salty gammon

1 tbsp olive oil
1 onion, diced
1 carrot, peeled and diced
500g yellow split peas, soaked
overnight in cold water
1.4kg smoked gammon
2 bay leaves
2 tbsp malt vinegar (or to taste)
25g unsalted butter, cubed
1 tbsp English mustard powder
2 tbsp demerara sugar

Serves 6
Prep time: 20 mins, plus
overnight soaking
Cook time: 2¼ hours

....

Per serving
469 cals, 15.4g fat, 6.1g sat fat,
10.8g total sugars, 4.7g salt

1 Heat the oil in a very large, deep, lidded saucepan. Add the onion and carrot, and fry over a medium heat for 3-4 minutes, until softened but not coloured.

2 Drain and rinse the soaked split peas and tip into the saucepan with the onion and carrot. Add the gammon and bay leaves, and cover with cold water. Bring to the boil and skim off any foam that rises to the surface. Turn down the heat, cover with a lid and cook over a low heat for 1½ hours, until the peas are tender and the gammon is cooked.

3 Drain the peas and gammon, reserving the cooking liquid and discarding the bay leaves. Set the gammon aside. Pour the peas into a food processor, add a few spoonfuls of the reserved cooking liquid and blend until smooth and not too thick. Tip into a clean pan and season to taste with salt and freshly ground black pepper. Add the vinegar and butter, beating well until incorporated. Set aside and keep warm.

4 Preheat the oven to 200°C, fan 180°C, gas 6. Remove the rind from the gammon, leaving a nice layer of fat on the top. Using a sharp knife, score diamond shapes into the fat. Mix together the mustard, sugar and 1 tbsp hot water to make a thick paste, then pour over the scored gammon. Place on a baking tray and cook in the oven for 20 minutes, until golden brown on top.

5 Thickly slice the gammon and serve with generous spoonfuls of pease pudding. Great also served with hot parsley sauce.

Give peas a chance

The British have an enduring love of peas and their appeal dates back centuries - they were easy to grow and could be dried and preserved, making them ideal peasant food. Pease pudding (or pease porridge as it was also known) was made from dried peas and its mild taste went down well with a hunk of salted bacon. Later variations added more flavour, such as sugar, pepper and sometimes mint. It's thought that the 18th century nursery rhyme 'pease pudding hot, pease pudding cold, pease pudding in the pot nine days old' refers to a form of the pudding that was left to ferment over several days. Mmm, sounds lovely ...

Pan haggerty

**You can't beat the comfort factor of thinly sliced potatoes
and onions sizzled together with cheese in a pan**

2 tbsp sunflower oil
2 onions, finely sliced
6 medium Maris Piper potatoes,
peeled and finely sliced
250ml hot chicken or vegetable
stock
125g mature Cheddar, grated

Serves 6
Prep time: 20 mins
Cook time: 40 mins
....

Per serving
298 cals, 11.3g fat, 5g sat fat,
4.5g total sugars, 0.4g salt

1 Heat 1 tbsp sunflower oil in a large, ovenproof, lidded sauté pan over a medium heat. Add the onions and fry for 10 minutes, until softened but not coloured. Remove from the pan and set aside.

2 Heat the remaining 1 tbsp oil in the pan and arrange half the potatoes in an even layer, overlapping, in the pan. Top with the cooked onions and, finally, the rest of the potatoes, seasoning with salt and freshly ground black pepper between each layer. Pour the hot stock over the top, place over a medium heat and bring to the boil. Cover with a lid and simmer for 15-20 minutes, until just tender.

3 Preheat the grill to high.

4 Remove the lid, sprinkle over the cheese, then grill for 5-7 minutes, until the cheese is bubbling and golden brown.

5 Spoon the pan haggerty onto serving plates. Great served with crusty bread.

Spuds you'll like

Potatoes hold a special place in the nation's heart and every regional cuisine seems to offer its own humble way of cooking these earthy staples. Pan haggerty, cooked in one heavy pan, dates back to the Industrial Revolution, when it was a cheap and delicious way to fill the bellies of workers in the old pit towns of Northumberland. This rustic dish has been gentrified over time and you'll now find versions including bacon, ham or sausage.

To serve...

Pan haggerty is great for veggies, or you could serve it with sausages or bacon

Rising stars

It is one of the miracles of English cookery that a simple batter, cooked in smoking hot fat, transforms into the deliciousness that is Yorkshire pudding. The first known recipe is for 'dripping pudding', found in *The Whole Duty of a Woman* published in 1737, and calls for the pudding to be placed beneath a spit-roast joint to cook in its dripping. Yorkshire cooks insist that only they can make proper Yorkshires – crisp and well risen – and, indeed, even Mrs Beeton omitted the fundamental rule of a hot oven in her recipe.

Yorkshire puddings

Traditionally eaten as a first course before meat to take the edge off an appetite,
Yorkshire puds are perfect served with roast beef or even enjoyed as a dessert

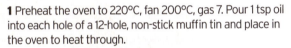

12 tsp vegetable oil
150g plain flour
¼ tsp salt
4 medium eggs, beaten
200ml semi-skimmed milk

Makes 12
Prep time: 10 mins
Cook time: 20 mins

Per Yorkshire pud
110 cals, 5.6g fat,
1.1g sat fat, 1g total
sugars, 0.2g salt

1 Preheat the oven to 220°C, fan 200°C, gas 7. Pour 1 tsp oil into each hole of a 12-hole, non-stick muffin tin and place in the oven to heat through.

2 Meanwhile, sift the flour and salt into a large bowl and make a well in the centre. Beat in the eggs until smooth, then gradually add the milk, whisking until the mixture has no lumps.

3 Pour the batter into a jug. Remove the tin from the oven and carefully pour the batter into the compartments. Return to the oven and cook for about 20 minutes, until the puddings have risen and are golden in colour. Serve immediately.

Sweet Yorkshire pud

Preheat the oven to 220°C, fan 200°C, gas 7. Heat a 1-litre roasting tin in the oven for 15 minutes. In a jug, whisk 225ml semi-skimmed milk with 3 large eggs. Sift 115g plain flour into a large bowl, stir in ¼ tsp salt and 1 tbsp caster sugar, and make a well in the middle. Add the milk mixture gradually, whisking until smooth and thick, then rest for 10 minutes. Melt 30g butter in a sauté pan and fry 8 halved, stoned plums for 2-3 minutes on each side. Add 3 tbsp light brown soft sugar and 2 tsp vanilla extract, and stir until melted. Brush the hot tin with 15g melted unsalted butter. Tip in the plums and sugary butter, spread out evenly, then pour over the batter. Bake for 20 minutes, until risen and golden. Great with cream.

Serves 6
Prep time: 15 mins   Cook time: 25 mins

Per serving 279 cals, 10.8g fat, 5.2g sat fat, 22.1g total sugars, 0.5g salt

Painted on numerous occasions by JMW Turner, Dunstanburgh Castle in Northumberland dates back to the 1300s

'O land beloved, where nought of legend's dream Outshines the truth'

Algernon Charles Swinburne

Lancashire hotpot

Slow-cooked lamb topped with slices of crisp, golden potato – no wonder this recipe has gone down in the history books as a classic

2 tbsp sunflower oil
900g diced lamb
4 lambs' kidneys, from the meat counter, cored, skinned and chopped
3 onions, halved and sliced
1 tbsp flour
600ml hot lamb stock
2 tsp Worcestershire sauce
1 bay leaf
3 sprigs fresh thyme, leaves picked
850g potatoes, Maris Piper or King Edward, peeled and cut into 5mm-thick slices
30g unsalted butter, melted

Serves 4
Prep time: 20 mins
Cook time: 2½ hours

Per serving
1041 cals, 57.1g fat, 25.5g sat fat, 8.9g total sugars, 0.2g salt

1 Preheat the oven to 180°C, fan 160°C, gas 4.

2 Heat 1 tbsp oil in a large frying pan and brown the lamb in batches over a high heat. Remove and place in a large shallow casserole dish. Add the kidneys to the pan, quickly brown them, then add to the lamb.

3 Heat the remaining 1 tbsp oil in the pan, then fry the onions over a low heat for 10 minutes, until golden brown. Stir in the flour, then add the stock and Worcestershire sauce, and bring to the boil, stirring. Season to taste with salt and freshly ground black pepper. Add the bay leaf and thyme, then pour into the casserole dish over the lamb.

4 Arrange the potato slices on top of the meat and brush with the melted butter. Cover with a tight-fitting lid and cook in the oven for 1½ hours. Remove the lid and cook for a further 35 minutes, until the potatoes are golden and crisp. Great with steamed green vegetables.

Top tip...
Sprinkle grated cheese over the potatoes for the last 35 minutes of cooking

Some like it hot...

This legendary slow-cooked dish has countless variations, with some recipes calling for kidneys, black pudding and even oysters. Traditionally cooked in a steep-sided stoneware dish (hence the name), it became synonymous with *Coronation Street*'s beloved barmaid Betty Williams (pictured), having been on the menu at the Rovers Return for nigh on 40 years. The late Betty Driver, who played the character, confessed she'd never actually made the dish herself because she didn't eat meat.

Flaky pastry encases a richly spiced fruit filling

Eccles cakes

It all began with a recipe involving a calf's foot filling (the less said, the better), but Eccles cakes are now one of Britain's most famous sweet treats

For the filling
15g unsalted butter, softened
50g light brown soft sugar
½ tsp ground cinnamon
75g currants
25g mixed peel
¼ tsp freshly ground nutmeg
Zest of ½ orange

For the pastry
1 x 500g block Sainsbury's puff pastry
Flour, for dusting
1 medium egg, beaten
1 tbsp caster sugar

Makes 12
Prep time: 20 mins
Cook time: 25 mins

Per cake
233 cals, 12.8g fat, 6.4g sat fat, 12g total sugars, 0.3g salt

V **45 mins**

1 Preheat the oven to 180°C, fan 160°C, gas 4.

2 Mix all the ingredients for the filling together in a small bowl.

3 Roll out the puff pastry on a floured surface to a thickness of about 3mm. Using a 10cm round cutter, cut out 12 discs.

4 Place 1 heaped tsp of the filling in the centre of each disc. Brush the edges with a little beaten egg and draw the pastry together to make a purse, squeezing tightly to seal.

5 Using the palm of your hand, flatten each cake until you can see the currants through the pastry. Place on a baking tray, sealed side down. Brush with more beaten egg, then sprinkle with caster sugar. Using a sharp knife, make 3 parallel cuts on top.

6 Bake for 20–25 minutes, until the pastry is golden. Leave to cool on a wire rack. Great served either warm or cold with a cup of tea.

Currant affairs

Probably more famous than the town from which it comes, the Eccles cake began its rise to popularity in the 1790s in what is now part of Greater Manchester, where bakers James Birch and his apprentice-turned-rival William Bradburn battled for supremacy in the apparently fiercely competitive fruitcake market. Small, round patties of flaky pastry with a currant filling, they're not to be confused with the similar-looking Chorley cake (less sweet) or Banbury cake (more oval). Today Eccles cakes hold a special place in the nation's heart, which not even their unappetising nickname – 'dead fly pies' – can diminish.

Yorkshire parkin

This delicious gingerbread is best made a few days in advance to allow it to become irresistibly sticky and chewy, but the trick is resisting it for that long...

150g unsalted butter, plus extra
for greasing
100g dark muscovado sugar
200g golden syrup
2 rounded tbsp black treacle
150g self-raising flour, sifted
175g medium oatmeal
2 tsp ground ginger
½ tsp ground mixed spice
2 medium eggs, beaten

Serves 9
Prep time: 15 mins
**Cook time: 1 hour, plus
cooling and setting time**

Per serving
**422 cals, 17.4g fat, 9.7g sat fat,
32.8g total sugars, 0.4g salt**

1 Preheat the oven to 160°C, fan 140°C, gas 3. Grease a 20cm square cake tin and line with baking parchment.

2 Gently melt the butter, sugar, syrup and treacle in a saucepan, then remove from the heat and leave to cool for 15 minutes.

3 Meanwhile, mix together the flour, oatmeal and spices in a large bowl. Pour in the cooled syrup mixture and eggs, then stir until smooth.

4 Pour into the prepared tin and bake in the oven for 50 minutes–1 hour, until a skewer inserted into the middle comes out clean and the top looks sticky. Leave to cool for 20 minutes, then remove from the tin and wrap in foil. Ideally, set aside in a cool place for a few days to become moist and sticky. If you simply can't wait to tuck in, leave to cool in the tin for 20 minutes, then turn out onto a wire rack to cool completely. Cut into squares to serve.

Top tip...
For a comforting pudding, serve with a dollop of warm custard

Flaming tasty

A mouthwatering combo of oatmeal and black treacle sets the Yorkshire parkin apart from its more southerly gingerbread cousins. Parkin is traditionally enjoyed around a bonfire on 5 November, to commemorate the attempt by one of York's sons, Guy Fawkes, to blow up the Houses of Parliament in 1605. One place that might not remember, remember the fifth of November in this fashion is St Peter's School in York, where Guy Fawkes was educated – a headmaster is reported to have decreed, 'We do not burn effigies of old boys'. The tradition of cake and bonfires dates back further, as the Vikings ate 'Thar' cakes and held bonfires to celebrate the feast of their god Thor.

Barn Hill, Stamford,
Lincolnshire

The best of
the Midlands

The Midlands

The Midlands

From the Peak District to the Lincolnshire Wolds, and the bustling cities of Birmingham and Leicester to the quiet villages of Northamptonshire and Herefordshire, the East and West Midlands are regions of great diversity – and that extends to their food

Occupying a prime spot in the centre of England, the Midlands stretches from the Welsh borders to the Lincolnshire coast. In addition to its chocolate-making heritage (in 1824 John Cadbury opened his first shop in Birmingham), the region has acquired a reputation for fine fare.

Melton Mowbray, in the East Midlands, is famous for its pork pies and is also one of only a handful of towns permitted to call its cheese Stilton – both foodstuffs have been awarded EU protection status so can't be made anywhere else. The Midlands is also the place to come for a chunk of Red Leicester or Lincolnshire Poacher.

From the Cotswolds to Worcestershire, this neck of the woods has perfect agricultural conditions for growing soft fruit, apples and pears in abundance, with refreshing perry a speciality of the region. Staffordshire, in the West Midlands, meanwhile, is renowned for its sought-after Tamworth pigs and its oatcakes, which, in this case, are pancakes that are served with fruit or jam, or even with eggs and bacon.

For authentic gingerbread, head for Ashbourne in Derbyshire, where it is still made to the same recipe brought to the town by French prisoners held captive there during the Napoleonic Wars.

5 foods the area is famous for

Melton Mowbray pork pie The real thing has a hot-water crust, bowed sides, a chopped grey pork filling and plenty of jelly.

Stilton Only five dairies in the world are licensed to make the delicious blue-veined 'king of cheeses', and they're all in the Midlands.

Hereford beef This native breed of cattle is revered for its naturally marbled, flavoursome meat.

Bakewell tart Is it a tart or a pudding? Whatever the correct name, there's no denying the deliciousness of this almond, jam and pastry combo.

Lincolnshire sausages These open-textured bangers are made from coarsely ground rather than minced pork, and seasoned with lots of sage.

Did you know?

Two Worcester chemists created **Lea & Perrins Worcestershire Sauce** in the 1830s. The recipe was devised for a local nobleman wanting to recreate the dishes he'd enjoyed during his travels in Bengal, but it wasn't to his liking. Months later, the barrels were rediscovered and, to John Lea and William Perrins' surprise, the contents had matured into the delicious sauce we still enjoy today.

The big cheese

Peter Hughes, production manager at award-winning dairy Tuxford & Tebbutt, has been making prized Stilton for 23 years. Overseeing a team of 40, Peter (pictured) ensures that each crucial part of the Stilton maturing process runs smoothly, from the milk intake right through to grading.

Tuxford & Tebbutt has produced Stilton at its site in Melton Mowbray since 1780 and each cheese takes 10-12 weeks to make by hand. With only five dairies in the UK licensed to make this 'king of cheeses', cheesemakers are very competitive. As Peter explains, 'Every dairy has to adhere to strict regulations, but we all have our own little tricks and secrets passed down through the generations.'

Peter's job involves daily tastings to ensure that the flavour is up to scratch. 'In my opinion we produce the best Stilton in the world. I wouldn't settle for anything less!' Pop into Sainsbury's to pick up a chunk and we're pretty sure you'll agree with him.

The British Asparagus Festival

Once a year, between St George's Day and Midsummer's Day (23 April and 21 June), the Vale of Evesham celebrates the British Asparagus Festival. The region's spears are among the best in the world, so expect to see many asparagus-themed events. Highlights include the Asparabus tour, a fortune-telling Asparamancer and a King of Asparagus competition. How very British!

Pork pie

Great picnic or pub fare, a generous wedge of pork pie offers the quintessential combination of moreish pastry, subtly seasoned filling and savoury jelly

500g pork mince
500g boneless pork shoulder, chopped
250g pork belly, chopped
250g streaky bacon, chopped
2 sprigs thyme, leaves removed and chopped
2 fresh sage leaves, chopped
¼ tsp ground mace
½ tsp ground white pepper
Large pinch of ground nutmeg
1 x 10g pack leaf gelatine
300ml hot vegetable stock

For the pastry
200g lard, cubed
580g strong flour, plus extra for dusting
Pinch of salt
Butter, for greasing
1 medium egg, beaten

Serves 16
**Prep time: 40 mins, plus chilling time
Cook time: 2 hours, 20 mins**

....

Per serving
479 cals, 29.1g fat, 11.6g sat fat, 0.6g total sugars, 0.8g salt

1 Place all the pork, bacon, thyme, sage, mace, pepper and nutmeg in a large bowl. Mix together well, then set aside.

2 Place the lard in a small saucepan with 220ml cold water. Bring to the boil, then remove from the heat and set aside until the lard has melted. Sift the flour and salt into a large bowl. Pour the hot lard and water into the flour and mix with a wooden spoon. Leave until cool enough to handle, but the pastry must still be very warm when rolling out.

3 Preheat the oven to 180°C, fan 160°C, gas 4. Lightly grease and flour a deep, 20cm round cake tin. Take about a quarter of the pastry and roll out to a 20cm-diameter circle for the lid. Roll out the remaining pastry to a circle slightly larger than the base of the tin. Lay it in the bottom and, using your fingers, firmly push it up the sides to the top. Check there are no holes or tears.

4 Spoon the pork filling into the lined tin and press down well. Brush the edge of the pastry with some of the beaten egg and place the lid on top. Press tightly to seal, then use the back of a fork to crimp the edge. Use the point of a knife to make a hole in the centre of the pastry to let out the steam. Place on a baking tray and bake for 30 minutes, then reduce the oven temperature to 160°C, fan 140°C, gas 3 and bake for 1½ hours, until the pastry is pale golden. Brush with beaten egg and return to the oven for a further 15 minutes, until deep golden. Set aside to cool completely.

5 To make the jellied stock, soak the gelatine for 5 minutes in cold water. Squeeze out the liquid, then add to the stock and stir until dissolved. Leave until almost on the point of setting.

6 Using a funnel, pour the stock a little at a time into the pie through the hole in the top. Leave to cool, then chill in the fridge overnight. Cut into wedges to serve. Great served with mustard.

A pie with a pedigree

The pork pie has hardly changed since the Middle Ages, especially that hailing from Melton Mowbray, which is baked free-standing and has traditional bulging sides. And as Melton Mowbray is one of the elite Stilton-producing regions, it really can stake its claim as the UK's rural capital of food. But the town has a more colourful history. In 1837, it is reported that a group of noblemen, merry after a hunt, daubed red paint on the townsfolk's doors - hence the description of a riotous night out as 'painting the town red'.

Shropshire fidget pie

Hearty and filling, fidget or fitchett pies were once produced all over the Midlands as a lunchtime meal for farm workers bringing in the harvest

750g shortcrust pastry
2 tbsp semolina
500g Maris Piper potatoes, peeled and thickly sliced
2 onions, finely sliced
50g unsalted butter
2 tbsp plain flour, plus extra for dusting
250ml whole milk
2 medium Bramley apples, peeled, cored and thickly sliced
2 tbsp muscovado sugar
6 fresh sage leaves, finely chopped
250g ham, cut into bite-sized pieces
100ml dry cider
1 medium egg, beaten

Serves 10
Prep time: 45 mins,
plus chilling time
Cook time: 1 hour, 40 mins

Per serving
585 cals, 32.1g fat,
18.3g sat fat, 11.9g
total sugars, 1.5g salt

1 Preheat the oven to 200ºC, fan 180ºC, gas 6. Set aside 125g pastry for making the lid later. On a lightly floured surface, roll out the remaining pastry to the thickness of a £1 coin.

2 Line a 23cm springform cake tin with the pastry, leaving a little hanging over the edge. Prick the base all over with a fork, then line the tin with baking parchment and fill with baking beans or uncooked rice. Chill for at least 20 minutes, until firm to the touch.

3 Place the tin on a baking tray and bake the pastry case for 15 minutes. Remove the beans or rice and parchment, then return the tin to the oven for a further 5–8 minutes, until golden. Set aside to cool slightly. Trim off any excess pastry with a small, sharp knife and sprinkle with the semolina to absorb any excess moisture.

4 Meanwhile, boil the potatoes for 2–3 minutes. Add the onions to the pan and simmer for a further 2–3 minutes, until both the potatoes and onions are just tender. Drain well and place in a large bowl.

5 Melt 25g butter in a saucepan, then add the flour and mix well to form a paste. Gradually add the milk, whisking continuously until smooth and thick. Pour the sauce over the potatoes and onions, season with salt and freshly ground black pepper and mix together.

6 Fry the apple slices in the remaining 25g butter until just starting to colour. Sprinkle over the muscovado sugar and fry for a further minute to melt the sugar and caramelise the apples.

7 Arrange the apples in an even layer in the pastry case. Spoon in half the potato and onion mixture, then sprinkle over half the sage and half the ham, and season with salt and freshly ground black pepper. Repeat until all the ingredients have been used, then pour over the cider, ensuring it doesn't bubble over the sides of the pie.

8 Roll out the reserved pastry to make a lid, setting aside a piece to make leaves. Brush the edges of the pastry case with egg, place the lid on top and pinch the edges together to seal. Cut a cross in the centre, decorate with the pastry leaves and brush with beaten egg.

9 Bake for 1 hour, until the top is crisp and golden. Set aside to cool for 10–15 minutes before removing from the tin. Cut into wedges to serve.

*The name 'fidget' comes from the Anglo-Saxon
for five-sided – the original shape of the pie*

Nottingham apple batter pudding

The first Bramley was grown in Nottinghamshire from a seed, so it's no wonder that this apple is the key ingredient in the county's best-known dessert

125g self-raising flour, sifted
Pinch of salt
3 medium eggs, separated
125ml whole milk
2 tbsp caster sugar
100g light brown soft sugar
50g unsalted butter, softened, plus extra for greasing
1 tsp ground cinnamon
2 tbsp brandy (optional)
4 small Bramley apples, peeled and cored but left whole

Serves 8
Prep time: 35 mins
Cook time: 45 mins

Per serving
240 cals, 8.8g fat, 4.8g sat fat, 23g total sugars, 0.4g salt

1 Preheat the oven to 190°C, fan 170°C, gas 5, and grease a 1-litre ovenproof dish.

2 Sift the flour and salt into a large bowl and make a well in the centre. In another large bowl, mix together the egg yolks, milk and caster sugar, then gradually whisk this mixture into the flour to make a thick batter. Set aside.

3 In a small bowl, mix together the brown sugar, butter, cinnamon and brandy, if using, until well combined.

4 Stand the apples in the greased dish. Stuff the sugar and butter mixture into the cores and on top of the apples.

5 In a medium bowl, whisk the egg whites until they form stiff peaks. Carefully fold into the batter, then spoon over the apples.

6 Bake for about 45 minutes, until the apples are tender and the batter has puffed up and is cooked in the centre and golden on top. Cover with foil halfway through if turning too brown.

7 Great dusted with icing sugar and served with cream or hot custard.

Number-one seed

For sweet, golden, fluffy fillings for pies or puddings, the Bramley pips other cooking apples to the post, and it's thanks to a young girl called Mary Ann Brailsford. In 1809, she planted the first Bramley's Seedling from a pip in the garden of her family's home in the Nottinghamshire hamlet of Southwell. Mary Ann lived in the cottage all her life and, after her death, the first grafts were taken from the tree by the local innkeeper, Matthew Bramley, who bought the house. In 1856, a nurseryman, Henry Merryweather (above), asked if he could take some cuttings, cultivate them and sell the apples. Bramley agreed, but insisted they must bear his name. The tree was blown down in a storm in 1900, but it survived and continues to bear fruit to this day. Not bad for a 200-year-old national treasure.

Bakewell tart

Moist, almond-flavoured sponge with a tangy layer of jam and soft, buttery pastry makes this traditional tart a wonderful treat served warm or cold

200g plain flour, plus extra for dusting
1 tbsp icing sugar
125g unsalted butter, chilled and diced, plus 175g unsalted butter, softened
1 medium egg yolk, beaten with ½ tbsp chilled water
175g caster sugar
3 medium eggs
175g ground almonds
1 tsp almond extract
200g raspberry or strawberry jam
25g flaked almonds

Serves 10
Prep time: 30 mins, plus chilling time
Cook time: 1¼ hours

Per serving
535 cals, 35.4g fat, 15.9g sat fat, 31.9g total sugars, trace salt

1 Whizz the flour, icing sugar and diced butter in a food processor until the mixture resembles breadcrumbs. Transfer to a large bowl, add the egg-yolk mixture and stir with a palette knife. Bring the mixture together with your hands to form a dough, adding an extra 1 tsp chilled water if dry. Roll into a ball, wrap in clingfilm and place in the fridge to rest for 30 minutes.

2 On a lightly floured surface, roll out the pastry to the thickness of a £1 coin. Use it to line a 24cm fluted, loose-bottomed tart tin, leaving 1-2cm hanging over the edge. Prick the base all over with a fork and place in the freezer for 10 minutes to firm up.

3 Preheat the oven to 180°C, fan 160°C, gas 4.

4 Line the pastry case with baking parchment and baking beans or uncooked rice, and place on a baking tray. Bake for 15 minutes. Remove the beans or rice, and return the tin to the oven for 10-15 minutes, until the pastry is golden. Set aside to cool, then use a small sharp knife to carefully trim the edges.

5 Meanwhile, whisk together the softened butter and caster sugar in a bowl until light and fluffy. Beat in the eggs, one at a time, with 1 tbsp ground almonds each time, then stir in the remaining ground almonds and the almond extract.

6 Spread the jam across the bottom of the pastry case. Pour over the sponge mixture and sprinkle with the flaked almonds. Bake for 45 minutes, until golden. When a skewer is inserted into the centre, it should come out clean. Remove from the tin and set aside to cool on a wire rack. Great served with cream.

Top tip...
Experiment with different flavour jams - strawberry or apricot will also work well

Accidental hero

Some say the Bakewell tart (or pudding, to give it its original name) was created by accident when, in 1820, a cook poured egg mixture on top of jam, making a tart instead of a pudding. However, other sources say it hails from a 15th-century dish called 'flathon', which was either a rich custard over a candied-fruit base, or made with ground almonds, sugar and spice. In its birthplace, Bakewell, you'll still find it sold under the name 'pudding'.

One of Warwickshire's most famous landmarks, the 17th-century Chesterton Windmill overlooks the village of Chesterton

'Shall I compare thee to a summer's day?
Thou art more lovely and more temperate'

William Shakespeare

Top tip...

For an extra twist,
add a handful
of sultanas to
the apple

Malvern pudding

The cooking apples in this comforting dessert add a tangy layer of fruit beneath the spiced sweet custard topping

THE FINEST APPLE ON EARTH!

BRAMLEY'S SEEDLING APPLE
See pages 6 and 7.

150g unsalted butter
1kg Bramley apples, peeled, cored and thickly sliced
125g golden caster sugar
Zest of 1 lemon
50g cornflour
800ml whole milk, warmed
2 medium eggs
50g demerara sugar
1 tsp ground cinnamon

Serves 6
Prep time: 30 mins
Cook time: 35 mins, plus cooling time

....

Per serving
517 cals, 27.5g fat, 17.2g sat fat, 50.5g total sugars, 0.3g salt

1 Preheat the grill to medium.

2 Melt 75g butter in a large frying pan over a medium heat, then add the apples and cook for 5–6 minutes, until softened. Add 75g golden caster sugar and the lemon zest, and cook for another 2–3 minutes, then transfer to a 1-litre ovenproof dish.

3 To make the topping, melt 50g butter in a large saucepan until foaming. Whisk in the cornflour and cook over a medium-low heat, stirring constantly, until a smooth paste forms.

4 Gradually add the milk to the pan, whisking continuously, until it has been incorporated and the mixture is smooth and creamy. Cook for a further 4–5 minutes, until thickened, then remove from the heat and set aside.

5 In a large bowl, mix together the eggs and remaining 50g golden caster sugar. Sieve the milk mixture into the egg mixture and stir well. Pour evenly over the apples.

6 Mix together the demerara sugar and cinnamon, and sprinkle over the top of the pudding. Dot with the remaining 25g butter and grill for 8–10 minutes, until golden and bubbling. Leave to cool for 10 minutes, then spoon into bowls. Great served with cream.

Pudding in peril

....

A recent survey listed Malvern pudding as one of the 10 most endangered puds in Britain, so it's high time we rescued it from extinction. Worcestershire is famous for its apples, so it comes as no surprise that this pud hails from that fruit-laden county. The pudding is a traditional baked dish that originated in Georgian times and is thought to be a variant on hasty pudding – a quickly made custard of milk, sugar, eggs and flour topped with sugar and spices. The residents of the town of Malvern tweaked the recipe, adding the apples that were plentiful in their area.

Lincolnshire steamed carrot pudding

This proper old-fashioned pud gets an extra boost of sweetness from carrots – long used by canny cooks as a plentiful source of natural sugar

100g plain flour
½ tsp bicarbonate of soda
1 tsp ground cinnamon
1 tsp mixed spice
75g light shredded vegetable suet
100g raisins
100g sultanas
200g carrots, peeled and grated
75g demerara sugar
100g fresh white breadcrumbs
30g glacé cherries, chopped
Zest of 1 orange
2 large eggs, beaten
100ml whole milk
Butter, for greasing

Serves 6
Prep time: 15 mins
Cook time: 3 hours

....

Per serving
414 cals, 12.3g fat, 6g sat fat,
42.6g total sugars, 0.5g salt

1 In a large bowl, mix together the flour, bicarbonate of soda, cinnamon, mixed spice, suet, raisins, sultanas, carrot, sugar, breadcrumbs, glacé cherries and orange zest. In a separate bowl, mix together the eggs and milk, then beat into the dry mix. Stir until well combined.

2 Spoon the mixture into a greased 1-litre pudding basin and level the surface.

3 Cut a sheet of foil and a sheet of baking parchment large enough to easily secure around the top of the basin. Lay the foil on top of the baking parchment and fold a pleat down the middle of both. Place on top of the basin, with the pleat in the middle, and secure with kitchen string, making a loop for easy removal.

4 Place an inverted heatproof plate in the bottom of a large saucepan, and put the basin on it. Pour in enough boiling water to come two-thirds of the way up the sides of the basin. Bring to the boil, then cover with a tight-fitting lid and steam for 3 hours, topping up the water if necessary.

5 When the pudding has cooked, carefully remove from the saucepan and leave to cool for 10 minutes. Remove the string, foil and baking parchment. Place a serving plate over the top of the basin, then up-end it and carefully turn out the pudding onto the plate. Cut into wedges to serve. Great with hot custard.

Top tip...
Serve as an alternative to Christmas pudding

*Savoury or sweet,
a steamed pudding is
the stuff of nostalgia*

The best of
East Anglia

East Anglia

The River Blyth at Walberswick, on the Suffolk coast

East Anglia

It's known as the 'bread basket of Britain', but East Anglia boasts a wealth of other famous and delicious fare – Cromer crabs and Suffolk ham, Fenland cabbages and the sea salt of Maldon are just a selection of the region's bountiful produce

With its long North Sea coast curving around Norfolk, Suffolk and Essex, East Anglia enjoys a wealth of fish and seafood. Sweet, meaty crabs are landed at Cromer, cockles are harvested at Leigh-on-Sea, mussels are plucked from the sea at Brancaster and oysters are raised in beds off Mersea Island. The sea also yields other treasures, such as samphire, an edible sea vegetable found around Norfolk's tidal creeks and treated as a delicacy, and sea salt, which has been panned off the Essex coast for more than 2,000 years and continues to be produced at Maldon today. Inland, the largely rural landscape is renowned for its agriculture. A large percentage of the farmland produces cereal, giving rise to East Anglia's reputation as the 'bread basket of Britain'. The Fens produce cabbages, celery and lettuce, while the Brecks and Suffolk Sandlings are suited to carrots and asparagus. The area is also well known for its quality meats – Norfolk for turkeys and Gressingham duck, and Suffolk for its ham. And the region's coastal marshes and flat fens also give shelter to game birds such as partridge, quail and pheasant.

5 foods the area is famous for

Crab Such is the popularity of this shellfish that it is celebrated in the Cromer & Sheringham Crab & Lobster festival in May.

English mustard This condiment with a kick is produced from seed grown in the bright yellow fields surrounding Norwich.

Norfolk Black turkeys A slow-to-mature traditional breed that delivers a deep flavour and more tightly grained, succulent meat.

Samphire Known as 'asparagus of the sea', this vibrant green marsh plant is usually steamed or boiled and served with melted butter.

Suffolk ham This regional speciality is cured with black treacle and stout for a distinctive flavour.

Did you know?

The Dunmow Flitch Trials Great Dunmow in Essex is home to a four-yearly ancient custom, in which a 'flitch', or side, of bacon is given to a couple from anywhere in the world who can prove to a jury of villagers that they have 'not wisht themselves unmarried again' in the previous year. Dating back to 1104, the trials are referenced in Chaucer's *The Canterbury Tales*.

Not just for Christmas...

With 23 years' experience under his belt, Mark Gorton of Traditional Norfolk Poultry is an expert on rearing healthy, happy birds. It was on woodland on Mark's organic farm that Sainsbury's Taste the Difference Norfolk Black, a traditional turkey breed, was first reared in 2005. The birds are free to roam outside as nature intended, in keeping with Mark's ethos, and given perches and straw bales to help keep them active. Originally known as Black Turkey, the Norfolk Black is believed to have been the first variety of turkey in Britain, having been brought here from Spain in 1524. It is slow-growing, resulting in a tender-breasted bird, and its plumage has a high oil content, which helps the meat stay moist. Black turkeys were present in the holds of ships making the transatlantic crossing from Europe to America, and were raised by early colonists. Ironically, it is likely that the turkey meat gobbled up at the first Thanksgiving meal may actually have been from a European bird, rather than one of the wild turkeys native to the continent.

Southend Whitebait Festival

There's more to Southend than amusement arcades – the Essex seaside town is also famous for its whitebait. This small fish is celebrated in the annual Southend Whitebait Festival, which is held in September and begins with the traditional ceremony of blessing the catch.

Potted crab

Before the advent of the fridge, potting meat or fish was a clever way to ensure it stayed fresh for longer – not that there's likely to be much left over after you've sampled this tasty treat

A really good catch

The sea off Norfolk yields a bounty of seafood and none is more prized than the crabs from Cromer, a Victorian seaside town in the north of the county. Smaller than those caught elsewhere in Britain, Cromer crabs are renowned for their sweet, tender flesh and high proportion of white meat to dark. There's no better way to enjoy them than with a dollop of mayonnaise, a squeeze of lemon and some buttered, crusty brown bread. The local catch is revered –

as well as appearing on menus all around the area, it is celebrated at the annual Cromer & Sheringham Crab & Lobster festival and is famous far beyond Norfolk's borders. Cromer has been supplying the country with shellfish since the early 19th century and, these days, the industry is still vitally important to the town. Cromer's delicious brown crabs are in season from spring to mid-winter, so get your claws into one when you can.

250g dressed crab
125g unsalted butter
A large pinch of ground mace
Zest of 1 lemon and 2 tbsp
lemon juice
A pinch of cayenne pepper
Crusty brown bread or toast,
to serve

Serves 4
Prep time: 10 mins,
plus infusing time
Cook time: 2 mins
....
Per serving
465 cals, 33.2g fat, 18.5g sat
fat, 1.3g total sugars, 1.3g salt

45 mins

1 Remove all the crab flesh from the shells and mix together the white and dark meat in a bowl.

2 Melt 75g butter in a saucepan, then remove from the heat. Stir in the mace, lemon juice and half the zest and allow to infuse for 10 minutes.

3 Stir the infused butter through the crab. Season with salt and freshly ground black pepper, then spoon into 4 x 100ml ramekins.

4 Melt the remaining 50g butter, then stir in the cayenne pepper and remaining lemon zest. Pour into the ramekins, swirling to cover the crab if necessary. Chill in the fridge for about an hour, until the butter has set.

5 Serve with crusty brown bread or toast.

Suffolk cyder mussels

This juicy dish of mussels in a mouthwatering cider and vegetable broth is just made for mopping up with lots of crusty bread

2kg fresh mussels
25g unsalted butter
1 onion, finely chopped
1 stick celery, finely chopped
1 medium carrot, peeled and
finely chopped
2 cloves garlic, finely chopped
300ml Taste the Difference
Suffolk cyder
½ x 28g pack Sainsbury's fresh
flat-leaf parsley, finely chopped
Crusty white bread, to serve

Serves 6
Prep time: 20 mins
Cook time: 20 mins

Per serving
319 cals, 6.6g fat, 2.9g sat fat,
4.7g total sugars, 1.7g salt

1 Scrub the mussels well in cold water and remove any beards. Discard any damaged shells or open shells that do not close when tapped sharply. Drain in a colander.

2 Melt the butter in a large, heavy-based saucepan with a tight-fitting lid. Add the onion, celery and carrot and fry gently, uncovered, for about 10 minutes, until lightly browned. Stir in the garlic and fry for 1 minute. Pour in the cyder and bring to the boil.

3 Tip the mussels into the pan and cover with the lid. Cook for about 5 minutes, shaking the pan a couple of times until all the shells are open. Discard any that remain closed.

4 Using a large slotted spoon, remove the mussels and divide between 4 bowls.

5 Stir most of the parsley into the pan, season with salt and freshly ground black pepper, then boil rapidly for 3-4 minutes to reduce the liquid slightly.

6 Pour over the mussels and scatter with the remaining parsley. Serve immediately with crusty white bread to soak up the juices.

To drink...
The zingy flavour of
Taste the Difference
Suffolk cyder
is great with
mussels

Nice mussels!

The saying that mussels are in season when there's an 'r' in the month holds true, and you can enjoy them fresh from September to April, depending how warm and early autumn and spring are. Brancaster Staithe, in North Norfolk, is particularly famed for this delicious shellfish, and signs outside many cottages proclaim 'mussels for sale'. They're well worth shelling out for.

Top tip...

Top crostini with teaspoonfuls of this pâté for perfect canapés

Smoked trout pâté
(with pickled cucumber)

This soft, buttery pâté made from smoked trout makes a deliciously easy starter, and the pickled cucumber adds a piquant contrast

1 x 125g pack Taste the Difference Scottish hot smoked trout fillets
1 x 120g pack Sainsbury's smoked rainbow trout
50g unsalted butter, softened
150g half-fat crème fraîche
1 tbsp horseradish sauce (optional)
Zest of 1 lemon
8g fresh chives, finely chopped
6 slices Taste the Difference multi-seeded wholemeal loaf

For the cucumber pickle

1 cucumber
2 tsp flaked sea salt
3 tbsp white wine vinegar

2 tsp caster sugar
½ x punnet Taste the Difference micro leaf garlic chives, chopped
½ x punnet Taste the Difference micro leaf pea shoots, chopped

Serves 6
Prep time: 15 mins, plus chilling time

Per serving
260 cals, 15.3g fat, 7.9g sat fat, 5.2g total sugars, 1.5g salt

45 mins

1 Place both packs of smoked trout in a food processor. Add the butter and plenty of freshly ground black pepper, and whizz until the butter has blended with the fish.

2 Briefly whizz in the crème fraîche, horseradish sauce, if using, and lemon zest. Season with freshly ground black pepper and pile into a dish. Scatter with the chopped chives, then chill in the fridge for 30 minutes.

3 Meanwhile, make the pickle. Peel the cucumber and halve lengthways, then scoop out the seeds with a teaspoon and discard. Slice the cucumber very thinly, place in a colander and mix with the salt and 2 tbsp white wine vinegar. Leave for 10 minutes, stirring once. Rinse briefly and pat dry on kitchen paper. In a large bowl, mix the sugar with the remaining 1 tbsp vinegar until the sugar dissolves, then season with freshly ground black pepper. Add the cucumber and chill in the fridge until required. Stir through the micro leaves before serving.

4 Toast the bread, cut into quarters and serve with the pâté and pickle.

Best fishes from Yarmouth...

The simple idea of turning smoked fish into a paste to spread on toast originated in Great Yarmouth, Norfolk, which was once home to a huge and prosperous herring fishery. Bloaters, a type of smoked herring, were originally used in the recipe. At the height of the trade, so many boats were tied up in the Yare it was said you could walk across the river on them. Holiday-makers would take home souvenirs in the shape of a small wooden box marked 'A present from Yarmouth', containing the smoked fish. Makes a change from a stick of rock ...

Poacher's pie

As a lean, white meat, wild rabbit makes a great alternative to chicken. Pop it in a pie and you'll be rewarded with a meal that's as rich in tradition as it is in flavour

400g plain flour, plus extra for dusting
Pinch of salt
75g unsalted butter
75g lard
1 tsp dried mixed herbs
2 x 300g packs Sainsbury's diced rabbit
1 x 160g pack Taste the Difference oak smoked bacon lardons
3 medium potatoes, peeled and sliced
1 large leek, washed and sliced
500ml hot chicken stock
1 medium egg, beaten

Serves 6
Prep time: 20 mins, plus resting time
Cook time: 2 hours

Per serving
703 cals, 34.5g fat, 16.3g sat fat, 2.2g total sugars, 3.7g salt

1 Sift 340g flour and the salt into a large bowl. Using your fingertips, rub in the butter and lard until the mixture resembles breadcrumbs. Add 5-6 tbsp cold water and use a table knife to bring it together to form a dough, then wrap in clingfilm and chill in the fridge until needed.

2 Preheat the oven to 200°C, fan 180°C, gas 6.

3 In a large bowl, toss the herbs and remaining 60g flour together with the rabbit. Mix in the bacon lardons, potatoes and leek, season with salt and freshly ground black pepper, then tip into a 2-litre pie dish.

4 Pour over the stock, ensuring it comes halfway up the pie dish.

5 On a lightly floured surface, roll out the pastry and cut out a circle that is slightly larger than the top of the pie dish.

6 From the excess pastry, cut strips wide enough to cover the rim of the pie dish. Using a little of the beaten egg, fix the strips to the rim. Brush with the egg, then carefully place the pastry circle on top to form a lid. Using your fingertips, crimp the edges to seal. Brush the pie with egg and cut a small hole in the middle to allow steam to escape.

7 Bake in the oven for 30 minutes, then reduce the temperature to 180°C, fan 160°C, gas 4 and cook for a further 1½ hours, covering with foil if the top is browning too much. Remove from the oven and allow to rest for 10 minutes before serving.

Run, rabbit, run!

Rabbit features widely in the cooking of East Anglia because the region was once home to a huge population of wild game. Ordinary folk, who could not afford farmed meat, were forced, under the cover of darkness and the threat of punishment, to poach – hence the name of this tasty pie. Inexpensive, lean and high in protein, rabbit has a subtle gamey flavour that can take the place of white meat in a recipe. Having recently been endorsed by celebrity chefs, sales have soared and it's back on the dinner table again – and sure to put a spring in your step.

The Backs, River Cam, Cambridge. The name 'The Backs' refers to the backs of the colleges of the University of Cambridge

'The chestnuts shade,
in reverend dream,
The yet unacademic stream'

Rupert Brooke

Roast pork loin
(with roast vegetables & homemade apple sauce)

Tangy apple sauce combines perfectly with succulent roast pork, and the crackling is just impossible to resist

1 tbsp salt

1 x 1.5kg pork crackling loin joint

1 x 1kg pack Sainsbury's Charlotte potatoes, halved

1 large bulb fennel, trimmed and sliced

1 lemon, sliced

2-3 sprigs fresh sage, leaves picked and chopped

2-3 sprigs fresh thyme, leaves picked

2 cloves garlic, crushed

2 tsp fennel seeds

100ml vermouth or white wine

3 tbsp olive oil

For the apple sauce

500g Bramley apples, peeled, cored and chopped

50g caster sugar

25g unsalted butter

Serves 6

Prep time: 20 mins, plus resting time

Cook time: 1 hour, 55 mins

....

Per serving

825 cals, 35.2g fat, 12.3g sat fat, 19g total sugars, 0.8g salt

1 Preheat the oven to 240ºC, fan 220ºC, gas 9. Sprinkle the salt over the skin of the pork and rub in well. Place in a roasting tin and set aside for 30 minutes.

2 Meanwhile, place the potatoes, fennel, lemon, herbs, garlic, fennel seeds and vermouth or wine in another roasting tin. Drizzle with 2 tbsp oil and season with salt and freshly ground black pepper.

3 Wipe the salt off the pork and pat dry with kitchen paper. Return the pork to the tin, rub in the remaining 1 tbsp oil and cook on the top shelf of the oven for 25 minutes.

4 Reduce the oven temperature to 180ºC, fan 160ºC, gas 4, and cook the pork for 30 minutes.

5 Place the potatoes and fennel on the shelf below the pork. Roast the pork and vegetables for a further 45 minutes.

6 Meanwhile, place the apples in a saucepan with the sugar and 150ml water. Cover, bring to a simmer and cook for 5-8 minutes, stirring frequently, until soft. Remove the lid and simmer until all the water has evaporated. Remove from the heat and beat in the butter with a wooden spoon or electric hand mixer, until smooth. Spoon into a serving dish and keep warm.

7 Increase the oven temperature to 220ºC, fan 200ºC, gas 7. Cover the vegetable tin with foil and continue to cook with the pork for a further 15 minutes. Remove the pork and vegetables from the oven and leave to rest for 15 minutes.

8 Remove the string from the pork and lift off the crackling. Carve the meat and serve with the crackling, roast vegetables and apple sauce.

Suffolk and Norfolk are both well known for their pig rearing

To drink...

The malty flavour of a pale ale would work well with this traditional dish

Norfolk plough pudding

Once served in January to mark the start of spring ploughing, this sausagemeat and bacon suet pud is now a year-round favourite

Butter, for greasing
225g self-raising flour, plus extra for dusting
Pinch of salt
85g light shredded vegetable suet
400g good-quality pork sausagemeat
8 rashers streaky bacon, chopped
1 onion, chopped
8 fresh sage leaves, chopped
1 tbsp light brown soft sugar
75-100ml hot vegetable stock

Serves 6
Prep time: 30 mins
Cook time: 3 hours
....
Per serving
550 cals, 29.9g fat,
13.6g sat fat, 5.6g total
sugars, 2.6g salt

1 Generously grease a 1-litre pudding basin.

2 Sift the flour and salt into a large bowl, add the suet and mix together. Gradually add about 7 tbsp cold water to make a soft but not sticky dough. Roll into a ball, tip onto a lightly floured surface and knead briefly. Cut off a third, wrap in clingfilm and set aside. Roll out the remaining two-thirds of the dough to a thickness of 1cm and use to line the pudding basin.

3 In another large bowl, mix together the sausagemeat, bacon, onion, sage and sugar. Season with salt and freshly ground black pepper. Place in the lined pudding basin and add enough stock to cover the meat filling.

4 Roll out the reserved pastry. Cut out a circle the same size as the top of the pudding basin, then place it on top of the pie, pressing the edges together to seal. Cover with a circle of lightly buttered, pleated baking parchment and top with a large sheet of pleated kitchen foil. Secure with kitchen string, making a loop for easy removal.

5 Place an inverted heatproof plate in a large pan and put the basin on it. Pour in enough boiling water to come two-thirds of the way up the sides of the basin. Cover and steam for 3 hours, topping up the water regularly.

6 Carefully remove from the saucepan and leave to cool for 10 minutes. Remove the string, foil and baking parchment. Place a serving plate over the top of the basin, then up-end it and carefully turn out the pudding onto the plate. Cut into wedges to serve. Great with mashed potatoes, thick gravy and seasonal vegetables.

Dig that pudding

This pudding was traditionally served on Plough Monday, the first Monday after Twelfth Night (5 January) and the day spring ploughing commenced after the Christmas period. Farm hands would drag a decorated plough around the streets, crying, 'Penny for the ploughboys!' It was an important way to earn money at a difficult time of year, and if landowners didn't pay up, they risked having their gardens ploughed. This traditional reminder of the work that goes into growing food on the land is kept alive today in the Essex town of Maldon, where the plough is paraded through the town accompanied by 'Molly dancing' by morris men.

Norfolk dumplings
(with savoury mince)

Simple to make, these traditional dumplings are light yet filling and go particularly well with mince

2 tbsp sunflower oil

500g lean beef mince

1 onion, finely chopped

1 large carrot, peeled and finely chopped

1 stick celery, finely chopped

1 tbsp plain flour

2 tbsp Worcestershire sauce

1 tbsp tomato purée

2 tsp dried thyme

500ml hot beef stock

For the dumplings

350g plain flour, plus extra for dusting

1½ tsp baking powder

Pinch of salt

Serves 4

Prep time: 20 mins

Cook time: 50 mins

Per serving

672 cals, 22g fat, 7.9g sat fat, 8.2g total sugars, 1g salt

1 Heat 1 tbsp oil in a large frying pan. Add the mince and cook until browned, then remove and keep warm.

2 Add the remaining 1 tbsp oil to the pan. Add the onion, carrot and celery, and cook until softened. Return the mince to the pan, then stir in the flour, Worcestershire sauce, tomato purée, thyme and stock, and cook for 25-30 minutes, until the sauce has thickened and the vegetables are tender.

3 Meanwhile, to make the dumplings, sift the flour, baking powder and salt into a bowl. Gradually add 250ml cold water in a thin stream, stirring well, until the mixture forms a light dough.

4 Turn out the dough onto a floured surface and knead lightly until smooth. Pinch off golf-ball-sized pieces and roll into 12 balls.

5 Fill a large pan with water and bring to the boil. Carefully lower the dumplings into the water, reduce the heat and simmer, covered with a lid, for 12-15 minutes, until they have risen to the surface.

6 Remove the dumplings from the pan using a slotted spoon and set aside to drain on kitchen paper. Serve the dumplings with the mince.

Top tip...
Try adding finely chopped herbs to the dumplings for extra flavour

Sink or swim?

Like Yorkshire puddings, Norfolk dumplings were intended to fill hungry diners cheaply, and disguise the lack of meat. When Great Yarmouth, Caister and Cromer were popular holiday spots for the masses, guesthouse landladies would frequently serve dumplings. Because they're light, these dumplings rise to the top as they cook and are known in Norfolk as 'swimmers'. Suet dumplings, in contrast, are disparagingly referred to as 'sinkers'.

Cambridge burnt cream

Debate still rages over whether the French or the British first devised the recipe for this irresistible dish. Let the experts argue it out while you get on with enjoying the mouthwatering combination of rich custard topped with crunchy caramel

Crème de la crème

The first recipe for crème brûlée may have appeared in a cookbook written by the French chef François Massialot in 1691, but Cambridge burnt cream – also made with double cream, egg yolks, sugar and vanilla – had already been on the menu at Trinity College for some 60 years, served with the college's coat of arms burnt into its crunchy top. Or so rumour has it - for even the dons at Trinity aren't entirely sure about its provenance. What *is* clear is that this seemingly uniquely French dessert has been enjoyed in Britain for centuries, although it wouldn't have included vanilla until the 1800s, when it became more widely available. If you prefer to stay true to the dish's historical origins, try substituting the vanilla with nutmeg or cinnamon.

100g caster sugar, plus 12 tsp extra for the topping
6 medium egg yolks
1 x 600ml pot Sainsbury's double cream
1 vanilla pod, split in half lengthways and seeds scraped out

Serves 6
Prep time: 20 mins, plus chilling time
Cook time: 50 mins
....
Per serving
609 cals, 53g fat, 31.3g sat fat, 28.5g total sugars, trace salt

1 Preheat the oven to 150°C, fan 130°C, gas 2. Place the sugar and egg yolks in a large bowl and whisk until pale and fluffy.

2 Pour the cream into a saucepan, then add the vanilla seeds and pod. Bring to the boil, then remove from the heat and discard the pod. Add to the egg mixture, whisking continuously, then strain through a fine sieve into a jug.

3 Pour the mixture into 6 x 150ml ramekins, filling almost to the top. Place them in a deep roasting tin and pour in enough hot water to come halfway up the sides. Bake for 30-35 minutes, until just set but still a bit wobbly in the middle. Remove from the water and leave to cool, then chill in the fridge for 2-3 hours.

4 Before serving, preheat the grill to hot. Sprinkle the top of each custard with 1 tsp sugar, then place under the grill to caramelise. When a thin layer of caramel forms, sprinkle on the remaining 6 tsp sugar and grill again to form a thick, crunchy layer. Serve when the tops have cooled and hardened.

The Southeast

Brighton Pier,
East Sussex

The best of
the Southeast

The Southeast

With an abundance of fertile land, an extensive coastline and great transport links, no wonder the most populated corner of the British Isles boasts a capital that ranks among the best in the world when it comes to food

The enchanting counties of the Southeast are home to some of the finest produce in England. Kent, 'The Garden of England', is fêted for its green swathes of land, sprinkled with ancient orchards, vineyards and breweries. Romney Marsh lamb is a seasonal highlight, as are cobnuts, jams, apples and pears. Fish and seafood also feature heavily, with oysters from Whitstable, delicate crustaceans and fresh Dover sole to name just a few.

Further afield, Hampshire oozes traditional rustic charm and farmers' markets galore. Magically coloured rainbow trout grace the River Test, which has kept local smokehouses in business for hundreds of years. And the leafy lands of the New Forest - a favourite hunting spot of William the Conqueror - boast a winning combination of sweet berries, wild mushrooms and prized venison.

And then there's London - one of the great food capitals of the world. Once a city of extremes, the diet of the Dickensian working class bore little relation to that of the upper classes. However, Victorian London saw the arrival of steam trains, which brought a steady supply of quality food to all. The railways hurried cattle, sheep and seafood from the counties straight to Billingsgate, Smithfield, Spitalfields and Borough markets - still frequented today by Londoners hungry for a bargain.

The River Thames also provided the key ingredient for the ultimate Cockney soul food of pie and mash. Eels, served either pickled or in a pie, teamed with mash and liquor (that's parsley sauce to you and me) is one of the last great Cockney culinary traditions. Cheap and filling, this surprisingly tasty dish is best washed down with a nice pot of rosy lee!

SMOKED MACKEREL $15.00 Kg

'Maybe it's because I'm a Londoner, that I love London so...'

Just add water

When it comes to watercress, the key is in the quality of the water, says Francis Holland (pictured), who oversees British watercress growing across Hampshire and Dorset for Vitacress.

'Wherever we grow watercress, there's a source of pure drinking water, usually from underground aquifers that come up to the surface through boreholes. We plant watercress into the gravel beds in February, starting with just a thin film of water. When the plants are established, we introduce up to three inches of water to support them.' Today, most of the planting and harvesting is done by machine, although the watercress beds are still rolled by hand to keep the plants compact and rooted.

The water acts as an insulator, giving a huge amount of protection from the cold weather in winter, and supplies the plants with lots of those nutrients that watercress is hailed for.

5 foods the area is famous for

Scallops Caught two miles off the coast of Rye, these succulent morsels are delicious pan-fried or roasted in their shells with garlic.

Watercress This green leaf grown in Hampshire bears the Latin name Nasturtium, which means 'nose twister', in reference to the plant's peppery tang.

Kentish cobnuts These cultivated hazelnuts have a fresh, delicate flavour and are great in stir-fries and salads, or roasted and rolled in chocolate.

Cherries Juicy, sweet and with a distinctive aroma, British cherries are the pick of the bunch.

Oysters EU-protected Whitstable rock oysters are among the best in the world. Detach from the shell with a fork to get off to a flying start.

Did you know?

Beigels, or bagels, arrived in east London with Ashkenazi Jewish immigrants who had fled from Russia and Poland in the mid-1800s. To create a chewy texture, the original recipe called for the hand-shaped dough to be boiled before baking. Often topped with sesame or poppy seeds, today these bread rolls are referred to as bagels but the original (and the best) beigels can still be enjoyed in London's Brick Lane.

The Isle of Wight Garlic Festival

Celebrate the potent bulb's versatility at the Isle of Wight Garlic Festival in August, and get to experience such delights as garlic beer and garlic ice cream. Minty chewing gum optional.

To drink...
A lightly oaked chardonnay will pick up on the haddock's smoky notes

Omelette Arnold Bennett

Softly cooked eggs and smoked haddock combine in this sublime omelette, which makes for a perfect breakfast, lunch or supper

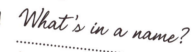

150g smoked haddock fillet, boned, skinned and cut into 4 pieces
250ml whole milk
2 fresh or dried bay leaves
6 whole black peppercorns
½ onion, chopped
35g unsalted butter
20g plain flour
½ tsp English mustard
30g mature Cheddar, grated
3 large eggs, separated
2 tbsp double cream
Watercress, to serve

Serves 4
Prep time: 15 mins
Cook time: 25 mins
....

Per serving
303 cals, 21g fat,
11.5g sat fat, 4.5g total
sugars, 0.9g salt

45 mins

1 Place the haddock in a deep frying or sauté pan with the milk, bay leaves, peppercorns and onion. Bring to a simmer and then poach for 7-8 minutes, until the fish is just flaking. Remove the fish from the poaching liquid and set aside. Strain the liquid (about 200ml) into a jug and set aside, discarding the bay leaves, peppercorns and onion.

2 Melt 20g butter in a medium saucepan, add the flour and stir until smooth. Gradually add the reserved poaching liquid and whisk until it is incorporated. Simmer for 1-2 minutes, then add the mustard and 15g cheese. Stir until the cheese has melted. Beat the egg yolks and stir into the sauce. Season to taste with salt and freshly ground black pepper, then add the fish.

3 Preheat the grill to high. Whisk the egg whites until soft peaks form, then carefully fold into the sauce.

4 Heat a 23cm non-stick ovenproof frying pan and melt the remaining 15g butter. Pour in the egg mixture and cook over a medium heat for 2-3 minutes, until the omelette has set on the bottom but is still a little wobbly in the middle. Scatter over the remaining 15g cheese and drizzle over the cream.

5 Place under the grill for 2-3 minutes, until just browning. Serve immediately with the watercress. Great with a hunk of fresh bread.

What's in a name?

Author and playwright Arnold Bennett (pictured) has been immortalised in this dish long after his works have largely been forgotten. While he was on one of his frequent stays at London's Savoy Hotel, during the 1920s, the chefs perfected an omelette for him made with smoked haddock, cheese and cream. The dish pleased the author so much that he insisted on it being prepared wherever he travelled. Omelette Arnold Bennett is a true British classic that remains on the menu at the Savoy to this day to commemorate Bennett's novel *Imperial Palace*, which he penned while staying at the world-famous hotel.

Watercress soup

This wonderfully spicy vegetable was once consumed by the Romans to cure baldness and by ascetic monks in Ireland for its purity. You can simply savour its tangy, peppery overtones in this traditional British soup

Not just a bit on the side

One of the oldest known leaf vegetables eaten by humans, watercress has been lauded for its nutrient properties since ancient times – an 80g serving is high in vitamin C and is a source of calcium and folate.

The English herbalist John Gerard hailed it as an antiscorbutic (preventive of scurvy) in 1636 and, according to the book *James Cook and the Conquest of Scurvy*, Captain Cook (pictured) was able to circumnavigate the world on three occasions partly because of the inclusion of watercress in his sailors' diet.

Watercress soup became popular in Britain during the 1700s when it was claimed supposedly to cleanse the blood, and the leafy green vegetable has been grown commercially in pure spring waters in the south of England since the early 1800s.

The soup enjoyed a revival in 2001, when the actress Liz Hurley revealed that she was a fan. In 2004, former Sex Pistols star John Lydon unexpectedly shared his watercress soup recipe with fellow contenders on *I'm a Celebrity... Get Me Out of Here!*

1 tbsp olive oil
1 onion, finely chopped
2 small potatoes, peeled and cut into 1cm cubes
2 x 75g bags Sainsbury's watercress
1.2 litres hot vegetable stock
2 tbsp crème fraîche

Serves 4
Prep time: 10 mins
Cook time: 35 mins

....

Per serving
129 cals, 6.9g fat, 3.1g sat fat, 3.1g total sugars, trace salt

1 Heat the oil in a large saucepan, then add the onion and cook gently for 5–10 minutes, until soft. Add the potato and cook for a further 5 minutes. Stir through the watercress, reserving a few sprigs to garnish.

2 Pour over the stock and simmer for 20 minutes. Using a hand-held blender, whizz until smooth.

3 Season with salt and freshly ground black pepper and serve in warmed bowls. Top each with a spoonful of crème fraîche and the reserved watercress.

'I've been walking about London for the last thirty years, and I find something fresh in it every day'

Walter Besant

Dating back to the 13th century, Borough Market, in Southwark, is one of London's largest and most vibrant food markets

Top tip...
The leftover cooked gammon is great in sandwiches or served cold with chutney

London particular

The gammon cooking stock gives this hearty ham
and pea soup a real depth of flavour

For the ham
1 x 750g smoked gammon joint
1 onion, roughly chopped
1 carrot, peeled and roughly chopped
2 sticks celery, roughly chopped
10 peppercorns
2 fresh or dried bay leaves

For the soup
30g unsalted butter
1 onion, finely chopped
1 carrot, peeled and finely chopped
1 small leek, finely chopped
300g dried yellow split peas

Serves 6
**Prep time: 25 mins,
plus cooling time
Cook time: 2 hours,
40 mins**

Per serving
**236 cals, 11.1g fat,
5.1g sat fat, 5.2g total
sugars, 2.4g salt**

1 Place the gammon joint in a large lidded saucepan with the onion,
carrot, celery, peppercorns and bay leaves. Add 2.5 litres cold water
(it should be enough to cover the gammon – if not, use a smaller pan).

2 Bring to a simmer, then cover and cook for 1½ hours, until the
gammon is tender. Remove from the heat and allow to cool in the liquid.

3 Remove the gammon and shred half the joint into bite-sized pieces.
Set aside the rest to cool, then cover and store in the fridge. Pass
the stock through a sieve, pushing the vegetables down with a ladle
to extract as much flavour as possible. Set aside the stock and discard
the vegetables.

4 For the soup, melt the butter in a large saucepan and gently fry the
onion, carrot and leek for 10 minutes, until softened. Add the split peas
and enough of the gammon stock to make up to about 2 litres. Bring to a
gentle simmer, then cook for 45 minutes, until the split peas are tender.

5 Tip half the soup into a food processor and blend to a purée, adding
a little more gammon stock if too thick.

6 Return to the saucepan with the remaining unblended soup and add
the shredded ham. Heat through until hot, and serve.

A real peasouper

The delightful name of this
thick pea and ham soup
comes from the so-called
'peasouper' fogs that used
to engulf London from the
1800s until the late 1950s.
These thick, yellowish smogs
swirled around as a result
of smoke from millions of
coal-fire chimneys mingling
with the cold, damp air of
the River Thames. The story
goes that it was a chef at
London hotel Simpson's-in-
the-Strand who gave this
toxic pollution a lasting legacy
of a much nicer sort in the
shape of this hearty, warming
broth, traditionally made with
green or yellow split peas and
ham. And resilient Londoners
took it to their hearts.

Eton mess

This all-time classic British dessert is one of the most delicious ways to celebrate that other summer favourite – strawberries and cream

3 large egg whites
180g caster sugar
1 tsp vanilla extract
500ml whipping cream
1 tbsp icing sugar
400g strawberries, chopped

Serves 6
Prep time: 20 mins,
plus cooling time
Cook time: 1½ hours

....

Per serving
489 cals, 32.5g fat, 20.3g sat fat,
40.6g total sugars, trace salt

1 Preheat the oven to 150ºC, fan 130ºC, gas 2.

2 Using an electric hand mixer, whisk the egg whites in a large bowl until stiff peaks form. Gradually add the caster sugar, whisking continuously until stiff and glossy, then fold in the vanilla extract.

3 Spoon large dollops of the mixture onto a baking tray lined with baking parchment, leaving space between each to allow for spreading. Place on the middle shelf of the oven, reduce the temperature to 140ºC, fan 120ºC, gas 1, and bake for 1¼-1½ hours, until firm to the touch. Remove and cool on a wire rack.

4 Whip the cream with the icing sugar until soft peaks form. Roughly break up the meringues and fold into the cream with 300g strawberries.

5 Spoon into 6 dessert glasses, top with the remaining 100g strawberries and serve straight away.

Try this...
Garnish with
a handful of torn
mint leaves for
a fragrant twist

Another fine mess...

Eton mess is traditionally served on 4 June at the prize-giving picnic at Eton College, and is reported to have been sold at the school 'sock' (tuck) shop since the 1930s. Myth has it that the pudding came about after a dog sat on a picnic basket, crushing the strawberries and cream inside. The Eton picnickers went ahead and tucked in regardless, enjoying the end result so much that they went on to recreate the pud. It's more likely, however, that the dessert's name comes from the now archaic meaning of 'mess' as a portion of food.

Chelsea buns

A favourite of George II and his grandson George III, these rich and fruity treats have truly stood the test of time

450g strong white bread flour, plus extra for dusting
1 tsp salt
1 x 7g sachet fast-action dried yeast
30g caster sugar
25g unsalted butter, cubed, plus extra for greasing
200–225ml semi-skimmed milk, warmed
1 large egg, beaten lightly

For the filling
125g dried mixed fruit
½ tsp mixed spice
60g light muscovado sugar
25g unsalted butter, melted

For the topping
2 tbsp runny honey
1 tbsp caster sugar

Makes 9
Prep time: 40 mins, plus rising time
Cook time: 30 mins

Per serving
345 cals, 7g fat, 4g sat fat, 20.8g total sugars, 0.6g salt

1 Grease a 20cm square, shallow cake tin with butter and line with baking parchment.

2 In a large bowl, sift together the flour and salt, then stir in the yeast and caster sugar.

3 Using your fingertips, rub the butter into the flour mixture until it resembles breadcrumbs.

4 Tip the milk and the egg into a medium bowl, and mix until well combined. Using a palette knife, stir into the flour mixture, a little at a time, until a soft dough is formed. You may not need to use all the liquid.

5 Place the dough on a lightly floured surface and knead for 10 minutes, until the dough is smooth and elastic. Roll out to a 35 x 25cm rectangle.

6 In a small bowl, mix together the dried fruit, spice and muscovado sugar.

7 Leaving a 2cm border around the edge of the pastry rectangle, brush the dough with the melted butter. Scatter over the fruit mixture and roll up the dough from the long side, like you would a Swiss roll. Cut into 9 equal slices and place in the cake tin, 3 in a row, cut-side up. Leave a little space between each slice to allow the dough to rise. Cover with lightly oiled clingfilm and leave in a warm place until well risen (about 45 minutes).

8 In the meantime, preheat the oven to 200ºC, fan 180ºC, gas 6.

9 Bake in the oven for 25-30 minutes, until golden. Drizzle with the honey and sprinkle over the caster sugar. Leave to cool slightly, then pull the buns apart and serve warm.

Chelsea morning

Created and sold exclusively at the Chelsea Bun House in Pimlico from the beginning of the 1700s, these glazed fruit buns were a big hit with commoners and royalty alike. In fact, the bakery was dubbed the Royal Bun House because King George III would frequently pop in for a Chelsea bun en route from the palace to the nearby Ranelagh pleasure gardens - where, according to Horace Walpole, the trendsetter of the day, you couldn't 'set your foot without treading on a Prince, or Duke of Cumberland'. The building was demolished in 1840, but the Chelsea bun tradition lives on at Cambridge cake shop Fitzbillies, where generations of undergraduates have enjoyed the sweet treat.

Top tip...

Use any leftover filling as a caramel sauce – great poured over ice cream

Gypsy tart

A Kentish school dinner favourite of yesteryear, surely this light and fluffy classic is long overdue a revival

300g plain flour, plus extra for dusting
150g unsalted butter, cubed
1 medium egg, beaten
1 x 410g tin light evaporated milk, chilled in the fridge overnight
280g dark muscovado sugar

Serves 10
Prep time: 30 mins, plus chilling time
Cook time: 40 mins

Per serving
382 cals, 15g fat, 9.4g sat fat, 31.1g total sugars, 0.1g salt

V

1 Preheat the oven to 190°C, fan 170°C, gas 5.

2 Sift the flour into a bowl. Using your fingertips, rub in the butter until the mixture resembles fine breadcrumbs. Add the egg and enough water (about 1–2 tbsp) to mix to a firm dough. Roll into a ball, wrap in clingfilm and leave to rest in the fridge for 30 minutes.

3 On a lightly floured surface, roll out the pastry and use to line a 23cm tart tin with a depth of 3.5cm, leaving any excess overhanging the edge. Line with baking parchment, fill with baking beans or uncooked rice and bake blind in the oven for 15 minutes. Remove the beans or rice, and parchment, and bake for a further 5–10 minutes, until golden. Leave to cool, then, using a sharp knife, trim the top of the pastry case.

4 Tip the evaporated milk and sugar into a large bowl and, using an electric hand mixer on full power, whisk together for about 8 minutes, until the mixture resembles a light coffee-coloured, creamy foam that doesn't quite hold peaks. For the best results, don't skimp on whisking time.

5 Pour the mixture into the tart tin and bake for 10–15 minutes. When cooked, the filling should be lightly set with a sticky surface. Leave to set overnight in the fridge. Great with a dollop of natural yogurt or crème fraîche.

Cook's note: it's crucial that the evaporated milk is chilled in the fridge overnight for the recipe to work successfully

Gypsy blessing

This sweet tart or pie is a very Kentish tradition and you'll find it in bakeries throughout the county. Many people associate gypsy tart with school dinners during the 60s and 70s when it regularly featured on the menu, probably due to its fairly cheap ingredients. While there is no hard evidence that it is a Romany recipe, legend has it that there was an old gypsy woman in a meadow who encountered a group of children looking so undernourished that she dashed home to look in her cupboards and made them what she could with what she had. *Et voilà*, the gypsy tart as we know it was born.

Sussex pond pudding

At first glance, this pud looks like a winter warmer, but the zing of a whole baked lemon inside will make you want to tuck in well into spring

250g self-raising flour, plus extra for dusting
Pinch of salt
125g light shredded vegetable suet
75ml semi-skimmed milk
125g unsalted butter, chilled and cut into very small pieces, plus extra for greasing
250g demerara sugar
1 unwaxed lemon

Serves 8
Prep time: 25 mins
Cook time: 4 hours

....

Per serving
466 cals, 23.3g fat, 14.3g sat fat, 32g total sugars, 0.4g salt

To drink...
The citrus notes of a muscat will chime nicely with the lemon in this pud

1 Butter a 1.2-litre pudding basin and line the bottom with a circle of baking parchment, then grease the parchment circle.

2 Sift the flour and salt into a large bowl and add the suet. Mix the milk with 75ml water and stir into the flour mixture to make a soft but not sticky dough. Knead for a few minutes, then break off a quarter of the dough and set aside.

3 On a lightly floured surface, roll out the remaining dough to a thickness of 1cm and use to line the basin. Leave an overhanging lip of 3cm all the way round.

4 Place half the butter and half the sugar in the bottom of the pastry-lined basin. Using a skewer, prick the lemon all over and place in the basin. Cover with the remaining butter and sugar.

5 Roll out the reserved pastry to a circle to make a lid. Moisten the edges of the overhanging pastry lip and the lid with water. Place the lid on top and bring up the overhanging lip to the edge, pressing firmly together to seal.

6 Cover the surface with a well-buttered circle of baking parchment, slightly bigger than the top of the basin. Cover with a pleated sheet of foil and secure with kitchen string, making a loop for easy removal.

7 Place an inverted heatproof plate in the bottom of a large saucepan, and put the basin on it. Pour in enough boiling water to come two-thirds of the way up the sides of the basin. Bring to the boil, then cover with a tight-fitting lid and steam for 3½–4 hours, topping up the water from time to time, if necessary.

8 When the pudding has cooked, carefully remove from the saucepan and leave to cool for 10 minutes. Remove the string, foil and baking parchment. Place a serving plate over the top of the basin, then up-end it and carefully turn out the pudding onto the plate. When cut, a rich lemon sauce will ooze out. Great with hot custard.

Hidden surprise

This glorious pud from Sussex is so called because the butter, sugar and syrup that fill the suet pastry case melt and ooze out into a caramelised 'pond'. This type of pudding predates 19th-century sponge puddings, but when the whole lemon was added is anyone's guess. Pricking the lemon lets the juices seep out into the pond, but sometimes it was left unpierced on purpose and exploded, causing the pudding to also be named 'lemon bomb'.

The best of
the Southwest

The Southwest

PW 240

Mevagissey harbour,
Cornwall

The Southwest

From verdant grazing pastures that help create award-winning cheeses and ice cream, to crystal-clear seas which are home to a treasure trove of fish, the Southwest is blessed when it comes to nature's storecupboard

The West Country is renowned for quality produce. Its rolling hills provide lush pasture for the dairy cows that graze there, so it's no surprise the area is famous for its cream, butter, ice cream and cheese. Regional cheeses include Cornish Yarg, a tangy cheese wrapped in nettles, Cornish Blue, which beat 2,600 entries to the title of World Champion Cheese 2010, and, of course, Cheddar. The Cornish pasty is known around the world. Intended as a hearty, portable meal to last local tin miners through the day, it often used to have a savoury end and a sweet end, giving the hard-working men a two-course meal in one handy handful. In the heat of the mine, the pasty's dense pastry would stay warm for several hours, but, if it did get cold, it could be warmed on a shovel held over a candle.

With its vast coastline, the Southwest is noted for its fresh seafood. A huge variety of fish is landed off the coast and local shellfish includes crab, mussels and scallops. Sheep and beef cattle are farmed throughout the region, and a relatively mild climate means a longer growing season for a variety of crops, including potatoes and strawberries. There are also a few surprises: tea is grown at the Tregothnan Estate in Cornwall, and the hottest chilli in the world is said to be the Dorset Naga!

Somerset's golden harvest

More than 100 years of expertise goes into the ciders made by award-winning producers Thatchers, in Somerset, who craft ciders for Sainsbury's Taste the Difference range. This family business was started in 1904 by William Thatcher, who built up Myrtle Farm from a smallholding and decided to produce cider. These days, Thatchers has developed into one of Britain's leading craft producers and the operation is headed up by William's grandson Martin Thatcher. Huge dedication goes into making sure the apples are picked at just the right ripeness for the perfect balance of natural sugars and acidity to create the best-quality cider. The cider is aged in 100-year-old oak vats until it is mature, to give it that special edge.

The family also likes to indulge in the ancient tradition of wassailing each January – a ceremony that involves blessing the trees, drinking cider from the wassail cup and having a bit of a knees-up. Now, that sounds like something worth celebrating.

5 foods the area is famous for

Cream teas Scones served with clotted cream and jam. For a Devon cream tea, you spread the split scone with cream and top with jam, whereas for a Cornish cream tea, the jam goes on before the cream.

Cornish pasty The traditional recipe is made with beef mixed with potatoes, onion and swede.

Apples Somerset is famous for its cider apples, which have been grown there since the 13th century.

Cheese There is a huge variety of regional cheeses to choose from, including Somerset Brie, Double Gloucester and Dorset Blue Vinny.

Wiltshire ham The traditional Wiltshire cure for ham has a long history dating back to the 1840s.

Gorge on Cheddar

Cheddar cheese has been made in the Somerset village of Cheddar since at least the 15th century, though there are references to it dating back to 1170. The cheese came about as people worked out how to use surplus milk in an age without refrigeration. By pressing the fresh curd with a heavy weight to squeeze out the moisture, it was discovered that the cheese lasted much longer. The local caves of Cheddar Gorge (above) provided the right humidity and constant temperature for maturation. This, combined with the rich pastures of the Somerset Levels, created Cheddar, now the most popular British cheese. These days, the name indicates a cheesemaking technique rather than the place of origin, as Cheddar is now made all over the world.

Cornish pasties

An iconic food of Cornwall, the pasty – a pastry turnover filled with beef and seasoned vegetables – is loved up and down Britain

500g plain flour, plus extra for dusting
125g slightly salted butter, diced
125g lard, diced
1 tbsp sunflower oil
1 onion, chopped
150g swede, peeled and diced
150g potato, peeled and diced
350g sirloin steak, cut into
very small pieces
1 medium egg, beaten

**Makes 4
(each pasty serves 2)**
**Prep time: 20 mins,
plus chilling time
Cook time: 1 hour**

....

Per serving
**656 cals, 39.7g fat, 20.5g sat fat,
3.2g total sugars, 0.5g salt**

1 Place the flour, butter and lard in a large bowl. Using your fingertips, rub together until the mixture resembles breadcrumbs. Add about 5 tbsp ice-cold water and, using your hands, mix to a firm pastry dough. Cover with clingfilm and chill in the fridge for 20 minutes.

2 Heat the oil in a pan and cook the onion over a medium heat for 6 minutes. Tip into a bowl, then mix in the swede and potato. Season with salt and freshly ground black pepper.

3 On a lightly floured surface, roll out the pastry dough and, using a 20cm plate, cut out 4 circles. Place a quarter of the vegetable mix on one half of each circle and top with the steak.

4 Brush the edges with some of the egg. Fold the pastry over the filling and crimp the edges with your fingers. Place on a baking tray lined with baking parchment, brush with more egg, then chill in the fridge for 15 minutes.

5 Preheat the oven to 200ºC, fan 180ºC, gas 6.

6 Bake the pasties for 10 minutes, then reduce the oven temperature to 180ºC, fan 160ºC, gas 4 and cook for a further 40 minutes.

To drink...
A fruity cider would go perfectly with the pasties' earthy veg and rich beef

In praise of the pasty...

Surely the Cornish pasty can lay claim to being the best portable working man's lunch ever invented. A filling of beef, root vegetables, potato and onion, encased in a pastry strong enough to hold by the crimped edge so his dirty hands didn't touch the filling? Perfection! For years, the pasty was the lunchtime fodder of farmers and, later, Cornish tin miners. Fillings varied depending on what was seasonally available and pasties of fish or just vegetables were also common. Tin miners who emigrated to the United States in the 1880s took their favourite lunch with them and Michigan is now proud to boast its very own Cornish pasty heritage.

To drink...

A dry cider will cut through the cream and complement the cider in the sauce

Somerset chicken in cider

This delicious casserole makes the most of Somerset's rich apple harvest, using both the fruit and cider in its sauce

1 tbsp olive oil
25g unsalted butter
8 free-range chicken thighs
1 onion, chopped
3 rashers smoked streaky bacon, cut into bite-sized pieces
2 sticks celery, chopped
2 tbsp plain flour
250ml dry cider
100–150ml hot chicken stock
2 Cox's apples, peeled, cored and sliced into wedges
1kg Maris Piper potatoes, peeled and quartered
2 tbsp chopped fresh sage leaves
100ml double cream

Serves 4
Prep time: 20 mins
Cook time: 1 hour

Per serving
764 cals, 34g fat, 16.3g sat fat, 12.5g total sugars, 0.7g salt

1 Preheat the oven to 200ºC, fan 180ºC, gas 6.

2 Heat the oil and 10g butter in a large flameproof and ovenproof casserole dish. Season the chicken with salt and freshly ground black pepper and fry in batches over a medium-high heat for 3–4 minutes on each side, until golden brown all over. Remove from the dish and set aside.

3 Add the onion, bacon and celery to the dish and fry for 5 minutes. Sprinkle in the flour and cook for 1 minute, scraping up all the sticky bits from the bottom of the dish. Add the cider, bring to a simmer and stir until thickened. Pour in enough stock to give the consistency of single cream.

4 Lay the apple slices over the bacon mixture, then top with the chicken. Cover with a lid and cook in the oven for 35 minutes – the chicken is cooked when the juices run clear when pierced with a skewer.

5 Meanwhile, place the potatoes in a pan of cold water. Bring to the boil, then simmer for 15 minutes, until tender. Drain and mash with the remaining 15g butter. Season with salt and freshly ground black pepper and keep warm.

6 Remove the chicken and place in a serving dish. Place the casserole dish back on the hob, add the sage leaves, then stir in the cream and warm through. Pour over the chicken and serve with the mashed potato.

Fruitful business

Somerset has an ancient history of apple growing and is still the country's major real cider producer. In the 18th century, it was customary for farm labourers to be paid part of their wages in cider. The Truck Act was introduced in 1887 to prohibit this practice, but it was effectively ignored. Somerset is also home to the notorious cloudy 'scrumpy'. This farmhouse-style, still cider can be pretty strong and tales abound of it catching folk unawares! West Country recipes have traditionally added a glug or two of the local cider to dishes, as it makes an excellent substitute for wine in cooking.

Bluebell woods on Bulbarrow Hill, Dorset. At 274 metres high, the hill offers spectacular views over five counties

'Oh! Roses and lilies are fair to see,
But the wild bluebell is the flower for me'

Louisa A Meredith

Dorset apple cake

This deliciously moist cake makes the most of one of Britain's best-loved fruits – the apple

225g self-raising flour
40g ground almonds
2 tsp baking powder
210g caster sugar
170g unsalted butter, melted, plus extra for greasing
Zest of 1 lemon
3 medium eggs
1½ tbsp semi-skimmed milk
400g Braeburn apples, each peeled, cored and cut into 8 wedges, then soaked in a little lemon juice
2 tbsp flaked almonds
½ tbsp demerara sugar

Serves 10
Prep time: 25 mins
Cook time: 1 hour

Per serving
378 cals, 19.3g fat, 10.3g sat fat, 28.2g total sugars, 0.5g salt

1 Preheat the oven to 180ºC, fan 160ºC, gas 4. Grease the base of an 18cm round cake tin and line with baking parchment.

2 Using an electric hand mixer, whisk together the flour, ground almonds, baking powder, caster sugar, butter and lemon zest in a large bowl.

3 Gradually whisk in the eggs and milk. Pour half the mixture into the cake tin and top with the apples, leaving any lemon juice behind. Spoon over the remaining mixture and sprinkle with the flaked almonds.

4 Bake for about 1 hour, until the cake is golden and firm to the touch, and a skewer comes out clean when inserted into the middle. Leave to cool in the tin before carefully removing. Sprinkle with the demerara sugar and serve.

Best of the West

Dorset is famed for its apple orchards, with varieties ranging from Golden Ball to Buttery Door, so it's no wonder that the county boasts its very own apple cake. Homemade cider, pressed apple juice and fruit jams have been produced from Dorset orchards since the 13th century, and ancient records show that monks were quaffing cider or 'cisera' at Shaftesbury Abbey as far back as 1291. Not surprisingly, Devon and Somerset also have their own versions of this afternoon pick-me-up, and similar cakes can be found sitting temptingly in bakers' windows throughout the West Country.

Scones

In Devon and Cornwall, folk argue over whether the cream or jam goes on first, but these West Country treats are winners however you serve them

350g self-raising flour, plus extra for dusting
Pinch of salt
1 tsp baking powder
85g unsalted butter, cubed
3 tbsp caster sugar
175ml semi-skimmed milk
1 tsp vanilla extract
½ tbsp lemon juice
1 medium egg, lightly beaten
½ x 227g pot Taste the Difference Cornish clotted cream
100g strawberry jam

Serves 8
Prep time: 20 mins
Cook time: 15 mins
....
Per scone
397 cals, 19.4g fat, 11.9g sat fat, 16.8g total sugars, 0.7g salt

1 Preheat the oven to 220°C, fan 200°C, gas 7. Place a baking tray in the oven to heat.

2 Mix the flour, salt and baking powder together in a large bowl. Using your fingertips, rub in the butter until the mixture resembles fine breadcrumbs, then stir in the sugar.

3 Heat the milk gently in a pan until warm, then stir in the vanilla extract and lemon juice. Using your hands, make a well in the dry mixture, then pour in the warm milk and mix together with a knife. Turn out the dough onto a lightly floured surface and gently fold over 2-3 times until slightly smoother. Gently roll out to a thickness of 4cm.

4 Using a 5cm cutter, cut out 4 rounds. Bring the remaining dough together and repeat until you have 8 scones. Brush the tops with the egg, then transfer to the hot baking tray. Bake for 10 minutes, until golden. Cool slightly, then cut in half and fill with clotted cream and jam.

To drink...
It's just got to be tea! See page 245 for how to make the perfect cuppa

Dream tea

Scones are found in various guises all around Britain. Earlier versions tended to be baked as one large cake and broken into wedges later – Northumberland's 'singing hinny' is one surviving example. Scones with clotted cream and jam is a match made in heaven – or, rather, in an abbey, as this teatime delight is said to have first been offered by the monks of Tavistock Abbey in 1105 to the Earl of Devon and local workers as thanks for restoring their monastery.

Cornish saffron cake

More like a bread than a cake, this Cornish speciality is very moreish – especially when served with clotted cream

150ml whole milk, plus extra if needed

2–3 large pinches of saffron strands

3 tbsp Cornish clotted cream

225g strong white bread flour, plus extra for dusting

¼ tsp salt

25g unsalted butter, softened, plus extra for greasing

7g sachet fast-action dried yeast

2 tbsp golden caster sugar

½ tsp ground mixed spice

50g sultanas

Vegetable oil, for greasing

1 tbsp clear honey

Serves 12
Prep time: 45 mins,
plus proving time
Cook time: 30 mins,
plus infusing time

Per serving
152 cals, 6g fat, 3.7g sat fat,
8.6g total sugars, 0.1g salt

1 Grease a long, narrow, 21.5 x 10.5cm loaf tin with butter and set aside. Heat the milk and saffron strands in a small pan over a low heat until almost boiling. Remove from the heat and leave to infuse for 15 minutes.

2 Add the clotted cream to the milk and saffron in the pan and return to a low heat for 1 minute to warm through. Meanwhile, sift the flour and salt into a large bowl. Using your fingertips, rub in the butter until the mixture resembles fine breadcrumbs, then stir in the yeast, sugar and mixed spice. Make a well in the centre and add the warm milk mixture. Stir well to make a soft dough, adding extra milk if needed.

3 Turn out the dough onto a lightly floured surface and knead for about 15 minutes, gradually adding the sultanas as you go, until the dough is soft and elastic. Place in a lightly oiled bowl and cover with lightly greased clingfilm. Leave in a warm place to prove until at least doubled in size (about 1 hour).

4 Punch the dough in the bowl to knock it back, then turn out onto a floured surface and knead for 5 minutes. Split the dough into 3 even portions and roll out to sausage shapes, just a little longer than the tin. Plait the dough together and tuck the ends under as you lift it into the tin. Cover with some lightly greased clingfilm and leave in a warm place until the dough has risen above the top of the loaf tin (about 30 minutes).

5 Preheat the oven to 190ºC, fan 170ºC, gas 5. Bake the loaf for 25 minutes, until risen and golden. Remove from the oven and brush with the honey. Leave to cool in the tin for 5-10 minutes, then turn out onto a wire rack to cool completely. Cut into thick slices. Great served with clotted cream.

Gold 'n' delicious

Saffron is the world's most valuable spice, worth more by weight than gold due to the sheer number of man-hours involved in its harvest and the tiny amounts yielded from each flower. Saffron comes from a special type of crocus, cultivated since ancient times in the East and believed to have been introduced into Cornwall by traders looking to exchange it for tin. Saffron's taste and intense yellow lends itself well to cakes such as this traditional bake.

153

Cornish fairings

With their distinctive cracked appearance, these spicy ginger biscuits have been popular for centuries

100g plain flour
Pinch of salt
1 tsp baking powder
½ tsp bicarbonate of soda
1 tsp ground ginger
½ tsp mixed spice
50g golden caster sugar
50g unsalted butter, chilled and cubed, plus extra for greasing
1 tbsp mixed chopped peel, finely chopped
3 tbsp golden syrup

Makes about 20
Prep time: 15 mins
Cook time: 8 mins

Per biscuit
61 cals, 2.3g fat, 1.5g sat fat, 5.5g total sugars, 0.2g salt

1 Preheat the oven to 200°C, fan 180°C, gas 6.

2 Sift the flour, salt, baking powder, bicarbonate of soda, ginger and mixed spice into a large bowl, then stir in the sugar.

3 Using your fingertips, rub in the butter until the mixture resembles fine breadcrumbs. Stir in the peel and the golden syrup, then mix to a firm dough.

4 Using your hands, roll the dough into about 20 small balls. Place well apart on lightly greased non-stick baking trays.

5 Bake in the middle of the oven for about 8 minutes, until golden. Leave to cool on the baking trays for a couple of minutes, then place on a wire rack to cool completely.

Fair's fare

The medieval equivalent of candyfloss, 'fairing' was once used to describe any edible item sold at one of the many livestock and labour fairs held up and down the country. However, over time, it became especially associated with gingerbread and biscuits. Cornwall's fairings, which originated at a 'maid hiring' fair in Launceston, soon became a staple at the yearly Whitsuntide and Corpus Christi gatherings, when they were given by suitors to their sweethearts to be enjoyed as they wandered, or kept as a keepsake. Enjoy with a cuppa – the country cousin of the ginger nut, the crisp, sturdy fairing is ideal for dunking.

Lardy cake

**This rich loaf from Wiltshire is a very naughty treat
for teatime, but a little goes a long way**

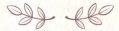

650g strong white bread flour,
plus extra for dusting
1 tsp salt
1 tsp caster sugar, plus 1 tbsp
to sprinkle
1 x 7g sachet fast-action
dried yeast
200g lard, softened
50g unsalted butter, softened,
plus extra for greasing
½ x 500g pack Sainsbury's
luxury mixed fruit
200g granulated sugar

Serves 20
**Prep time: 30 mins,
plus proving time
Cook time: 40 mins**
....

Per serving
305 cals, 12.7g fat, 6g sat fat,
20.7g total sugars, 0.3g salt

1 Place the flour, salt, caster sugar and yeast in a large bowl and mix together. Add 400ml warm water and mix to a soft dough. Knead on a lightly floured board until smooth.

2 In another large bowl, mix together the lard, butter, mixed fruit and granulated sugar. Divide into 3 portions.

3 Roll out the dough to a rectangle about twice as long as it is wide (50 x 20cm). Spread the bottom two-thirds with one-third of the fruit mixture. Fold the top third over the middle third and the remaining third over this to form a neat rectangular parcel. Give the pastry a quarter turn, then roll out to a rectangle as before. Spread with 1 of the remaining portions of fruit mixture and fold as before. Repeat the process once more, making sure, on the last rolling, that your dough is slightly smaller than a 20 x 25cm baking tray.

4 Grease the baking tray with butter. Place the dough in the tin, pressing it out towards the corners. Leave to rise in a warm place until doubled in size (about 1 hour).

5 Preheat the oven to 190ºC, fan 170ºC, gas 5. Using a sharp knife, mark the top of the lardy cake in a crisscross fashion. Bake for about 40 minutes, until well risen and golden. Turn out onto another baking tray to cool. Turn over and sprinkle generously with caster sugar. Cut into slices and serve warm.

Lardy by name...
....

Back in the 19th century, when sugar, spices and dried fruit were luxuries, this rich, sweet teacake would have been made from offcuts of the bread dough and eaten on high days and holidays, and at harvest festivals. The West Country is famous for its pigs and every part would have been put to good use, including, as here, the lard, which gives the cake a lovely moistness that is nicely balanced by the ooze of caramelised sugar.

The best of
Wales

Grongar Hill,
Llandeilo

Wales

Wales

With its dramatic mountainous uplands and rich pastures sweeping down to the sea, the magnificent landscapes of Wales provide a wonderful environment for a wide variety of culinary delights

Think of Wales and your mind inevitably wanders to lamb. This stunning landscape is perfectly suited to sheep farming, and the sheep that graze here produce some of the most flavoursome lamb that Britain has to offer. The changing terrain also results in a lengthy lambing season, with the warmer lowlands producing their lambs first and the hardier uplands following later, so we get to enjoy Welsh lamb nearly all year round. This is also a great environment for rearing cattle, and Welsh beef is highly prized. As a result, farming has been at the heart of Welsh food culture for centuries. As you might expect, traditional dishes centre around lamb, cheese and, of course, leeks – the national symbol of Wales.

The coast also plays an important role in Welsh food. One speciality is laver bread, made from boiled seaweed. This famed delicacy has been described as 'Welsh caviar' and is often blended with oatmeal and made into 'cakes', which are fried and served as part of a Welsh breakfast. Plenty of fish and seafood can also be found off the Welsh coast, including sea bass, cockles and mussels.

Visit Wales today and it's clear that the country hasn't lost any of its rural charm. You'll still find plenty of traditional pubs full of character, serving fine local ale and good, hearty food. Yet cool Cymru is becoming a foodie force to be reckoned with, and not just in Cardiff. The town of Abergavenny has plenty to offer hungry visitors and a growing gastronomic scene has sprung up. The Welsh are proud folk and when you sample their quality fare you can understand why.

Hitting the high notes

Pay a visit to Dafydd Edwards' farm, in the Cambrian mountain range near Bethania, in Cardiganshire, and if you're lucky, you'll hear not just the distant bleating of Dafydd's organic sheep, nor the chirping of the birds among the hedgerows, but Dafydd himself, singing *My Little Welsh Home on the Hill*.

With more than 1,500 acres of land and plenty of sheep and Welsh Black cattle to tend to, Dafydd and his wife, Anne, have had more than a little practice at farming. 'We have two or three places that have been in the family for many generations, a few hundred years,' Dafydd says. He joined the scheme Tir Gofal ('Land Care' in English), which rewards farmers who care for the environment. Of his decision to change to organic farming 12 years ago, he says: 'It's a natural and healthy way of living with the land. It's far better for human beings to eat organic, and organic lamb tastes so much better.' And that's something to sing about.

5 foods the area is famous for

Lamb and beef Wales has been granted protected geographical status by the European Union in recognition of its unique heritage, character and reputation.

Laver bread The edible seaweed laver is plucked from its rocky home and boiled into a green purée to create this Welsh delicacy.

Welsh rarebit An irresistible blend of ale, mustard and melted cheese – the Rolls-Royce of cheese on toast.

Bara brith Translated as 'speckled bread', this currant-filled spicy treat is delicious eaten warm with butter.

Glamorgan sausage This veggie classic combines leeks, cheese and breadcrumbs – with not a real sausage in sight!

Did you know? Both the Greeks and Romans of classical antiquity were rather fond of leeks, particularly Emperor Nero, who believed that eating the vegetable would enhance his singing voice. In fact he ate so many leeks, he was nicknamed Porrophagus, which means leek eater. The Romans introduced the vegetable to other countries, but something special happened in Wales. Legend has it that the Welsh adopted the vegetable as a national emblem in the 7th century when the Welsh army defeated the Saxons after wearing leeks in their hats to distinguish themselves from their enemy.

Abergavenny Food Festival

There's a gastronomic revolution happening in Wales, and Abergavenny is steering the way. Every September the Abergavenny Food Festival puts on a delicious show of the very best of Wales – from top producers to award-winning chefs – and each year it's getting bigger and better.

Welsh rarebit

**With the alchemy of ale, egg and mustard, a humble standby supper dish
is transformed into a tasty and satisfying traditional treat**

Rabbiting on

Believed to have originated in the 18th century, the intriguingly named Welsh rarebit originally had the ironic title of 'Welsh rabbit' - it was the food of the common man who couldn't afford the luxury of meat. In England the poor man's meat was rabbit, while in Wales, the poor man's meat was thought to be cheese. But the Welsh had the last laugh, as by the early 20th century, 'le Welsh' was all the rage at the Criterion restaurant in Paris, and was more often than not washed down with English ale served in a pewter tankard. The dish was traditionally made with Cheddar cheese, and variations with a poached egg – known as buck's rabbit – appeared later on. When Welsh rarebit is blended with tomatoes or tomato soup, it's known as a blushing bunny.

1 x 270g loaf Taste the Difference
ciabatta
20g unsalted butter
25g plain flour
125ml semi-skimmed milk
2 tbsp ale or cider
1 tsp English mustard powder
1 tsp Worcestershire sauce
200g be good to yourself British
mature white cheese, grated
1 medium egg, beaten
1 x 120g bag Sainsbury's bistro
salad, to serve
Taste the Difference spiced apple
& pear chutney, to serve

Serves 6 (2 slices each)
Prep time: 10 mins
Cook time: 10 mins
....
Per serving
322 cals, 12.5g fat, 6.1g sat fat,
9g total sugars, 1.4g salt

1 Preheat the grill to medium-high and cut the loaf into 12 slices. Grill until lightly golden on both sides, then set aside. Leave the grill on.

2 Melt the butter in a pan over a low heat. Add the flour and stir for 1 minute. Remove from the heat and gradually add the milk, stirring all the time. Bring to the boil, then add the ale or cider and stir for 1 minute. Stir in the mustard powder, Worcestershire sauce and cheese, then remove from the heat.

3 Stir in the egg, then spoon onto the ciabatta. Place on a baking tray and grill for 3–4 minutes, until golden. Serve hot with the salad and chutney.

Cook's note: this recipe contains raw eggs

Cawl

This classic broth, served with a hunk of bread and cheese, is the perfect thing to banish the cold on a blustery day

2 tbsp olive oil
2 medium carrots, peeled and chopped
200g turnip or swede, peeled and chopped
1 parsnip, peeled and chopped
1 large or 2 small leeks, washed and sliced
(keeping the white and green separate)
2 x 260g packs Sainsbury's lamb neck
fillet, cut into 2cm cubes
1 tsp peppercorns, crushed
500g potatoes, peeled and chopped
1 x 28g pack Sainsbury's fresh flat-leaf
parsley, finely chopped

Serves 4
Prep time: 15 mins
Cook time: 1 hour, 40 mins

Per serving
477 cals, 24.6g fat,
9.3g sat fat, 8.9g total
sugars, 0.3g salt

1 In a large flameproof casserole dish, heat 1 tbsp oil and add the carrots, turnip (or swede), parsnip and the whites of the leeks. Cook for 5 minutes, until lightly browned, then transfer to a bowl and set aside.

2 Heat the remaining 1 tbsp oil in the casserole dish, then add the lamb, in batches, cooking until browned on all sides. Return the vegetables to the dish, pour over 2 litres cold water and sprinkle over the crushed peppercorns. Cover tightly with a lid and bring to the boil, then reduce the heat to a simmer and cook for 1 hour.

3 Add the potatoes to the dish, then cover and simmer gently for 20 minutes. Add the leek greens and cook for a further 5 minutes.

4 Season to taste with salt and freshly ground black pepper, then serve in deep bowls with a generous sprinkling of parsley on top. Great with crusty bread and Welsh cheese.

One-pot wonder

This dish was traditionally cooked in an iron pot or cauldron over the fire. Its ingredients vary from region to region and even season to season, but lamb and leeks are always included, owing to their association with Wales. Cawl is generally eaten as a hearty one-course meal, often with bread and cheese, but in some parts the broth is eaten as a first course and the meat and vegetables separately as a second. Whichever way you eat it, the flavours improve with time, so don't be afraid to make it ahead, then refrigerate and reheat. 'Cawl' is derived from the Latin for 'stalk of a plant', and it rhymes with 'howl' rather than 'shawl'.

165

Glamorgan sausages

No chapter about Welsh food could overlook the leek, national symbol of Wales – here encased with tangy Caerphilly cheese in crunchy breadcrumbs

225g fresh white breadcrumbs
150g Caerphilly cheese, crumbled
1 small leek, washed and very finely chopped
1 tbsp chopped fresh flat-leaf parsley
1 tsp chopped fresh thyme leaves
1 tsp English mustard
2 medium eggs, lightly beaten
A little milk to blend, if necessary
2 tbsp sunflower oil, for frying
½ x 250g pack Sainsbury's baby plum tomatoes, halved, to serve
1 x 80g pack Sainsbury's herb salad, to serve

Serves 4 (2 sausages each)
Prep time: 20 mins, plus chilling time
Cook time: 15 mins

Per serving
400 cals, 22.4g fat, 9.7g sat fat, 4.2g total sugars, 1.3g salt

1 Place 150g breadcrumbs in a large bowl. Add the cheese, leek, parsley and thyme, season to taste with salt and freshly ground black pepper, and mix together.

2 Beat the mustard into the eggs. Add half the egg mixture to the breadcrumb and cheese mixture, and combine with your hands until it comes together. Loosen with a little milk, if necessary, then shape into 8 sausages, each about 2.5cm in diameter.

3 Pour the remaining egg mixture into a shallow dish and spread the remaining 75g breadcrumbs onto a plate. Dip each sausage into the egg, then coat in the breadcrumbs. Chill in the fridge for 30 minutes to firm up.

4 Heat the oil in a frying pan and cook the sausages, in batches, over a medium heat for about 5-8 minutes, increasing the heat towards the end so they become crisp and brown. Serve with the tomatoes and herb salad for a tasty light lunch.

A cracker of a croquette

Vegetarians can breathe a sigh of relief when they see Glamorgan sausages on the menu – Wales' best-known banger is meat-free! The main ingredients are cheese, leeks and breadcrumbs. The original recipe used Glamorgan cheese, made with milk from the Gwent breed of white cattle, but this cheese is no longer produced. However, sharp and crumbly Caerphilly is made to a similar recipe, so lends the same texture and flavour to this tasty dish.

167

Honeyed Welsh lamb

For a true taste of Wales, look no further than tender local lamb, famed for its flavour and succulence, and roasted here with delicious sweet honey

40g slightly salted butter, at room temperature

2 sprigs fresh rosemary, finely chopped

5 tbsp Taste the Difference Scottish heather honey

2 onions, sliced into 1cm rounds

2kg leg of Welsh lamb

400ml dry cider

2 tsp cornflour mixed with 2 tbsp water

Serves 6
Prep time: 15 mins
Cook time: 3 hours, 40 mins, plus resting time

Per serving
609 cals, 36.3g fat, 15.8g sat fat, 19g total sugars, 3.8g salt

1 Preheat the oven to 200ºC, fan 180ºC, gas 6. Mix together the butter, rosemary and honey, and season with freshly ground black pepper. Spread out the onions in a single layer in a roasting tin large enough to fit the lamb. Add the lamb, then brush with half the honey dressing. Pour in the cider, adding enough boiling water, if necessary, to ensure a depth of 1cm of liquid in the tin. Roast for 40 minutes, until golden.

2 Reduce the oven temperature to 180ºC, fan 160ºC, gas 4. Cover the lamb loosely with foil and cook for 2 hours, adding boiling water, if necessary, to maintain a 1cm-depth of liquid in the tin. Brush the remaining honey butter over the lamb, then cover loosely again with the foil and cook for a further hour. Remove the meat and place on a warmed plate, re-cover with the foil and set aside to rest for 15 minutes.

3 Meanwhile, strain the cooking juices through a sieve into a measuring jug. Press the onions to release their flavour, then cover the tin to keep them warm.

4 To make the gravy, skim off any visible fat from the juices, then add enough boiling water to make up to 400ml. Pour into a small saucepan and stir in the cornflour mixture. Simmer on the hob for a few minutes, stirring, then serve with the lamb, thickly sliced, and the onions.

Serve with...
Delicious with roast potatoes (see page 237) and tender broccoli

World-beating meat

Wales' unspoilt landscape has been home to native sheep for centuries - among them hardy mountain breeds - that have thrived on the abundant grazing available all year round. The much-prized meat has a good colour and a sweet flavour renowned throughout the world, and the farmers' traditional methods have earned them plenty of accolades. Indeed, such is the unique character, heritage and reputation of Welsh lamb that it has been recognised by the European Union and awarded the coveted status of Protected Geographical Indication. That really has put Welsh lamb on the map.

South Stack Lighthouse, near Holyhead, acts as a warning beacon to passing ships of the treacherous rocks below

'One road leads to London, one road leads to Wales, My road leads me seawards, to the white dipping sails'

John Masefield

Anglesey eggs

Nestle a clutch of eggs on a bed of mashed potatoes and leeks, smother in a cheese sauce and bake till golden. Irresistible ...

6 large eggs, at room temperature
600g potatoes, peeled and chopped
1 tsp Dijon mustard
3 tbsp whole milk
2 large leeks, washed, trimmed and sliced
20g unsalted butter
50g fresh white breadcrumbs
25g mature Cheddar, grated
1 tbsp chopped fresh flat-leaf parsley

For the sauce
30g unsalted butter
30g plain flour
400ml whole milk
1 tsp Dijon mustard
100g mature Cheddar, grated

Serves 4
Prep time: 20 mins
Cook time: 55 mins

Per serving
**640 cals, 37.6g fat,
19.4g sat fat, 8.6g total
sugars, 1.4g salt**

 V

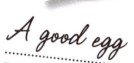

1 Place the eggs in a large pan of hot but not boiling water. Bring to the boil, then simmer for 7 minutes. Remove the eggs and place under cold running water until cool enough to handle. Peel, cut in half and set aside.

2 Place the potatoes in a pan of cold water. Bring to the boil, then simmer for 12-15 minutes, until tender. Drain, mash until smooth, then mix in the mustard and milk. Season with salt and freshly ground black pepper, then set aside and keep warm.

3 Meanwhile, fry the leeks in the butter for 3-4 minutes, until tender. Stir into the mashed potatoes.

4 Preheat the oven to 200°C, fan 180°C, gas 6. Mix together the breadcrumbs, cheese and parsley for the topping, and set aside.

5 For the sauce, melt the butter in a pan over a low heat and whisk in the flour. Gradually add the milk, whisking for 4-5 minutes, until thick and smooth. Stir in the mustard and cheese until melted. Season to taste with salt and freshly ground black pepper.

6 Spoon the mash in an even layer into a 24cm-square ovenproof dish. Top with the eggs, cut-side up, then pour over the sauce and scatter on the breadcrumb topping. Place on a baking tray and bake for 20-25 minutes, until golden and bubbling.

A good egg

The isle of Anglesey, separated from North Wales by the Menai Strait, has more than one fine egg tradition: the recipe on this page, which is a simple and tasty way of using up leftover potatoes and chunks of cheese, and an ancient Easter custom called *clepian wyau*. The latter took place on the Monday before Easter, when children would visit their neighbours to ask for eggs, chanting, '*Clap, clap, gofyn wy, i hogia' bach ar y plwy*' - 'Clap, clap, we ask for an egg, for the little children of the parish' - while making a clapping noise with wooden clappers. The most successful could collect as many as 200 to take home to their mothers!

Welsh cakes

A frugal feast to brighten up breakfast or tempt at teatime, this popular recipe has been passed down with little change through the generations

225g self-raising flour, plus extra for dusting
1 tsp mixed spice
Pinch of salt
125g unsalted butter, cubed
80g currants
Zest of ½ lemon
100g caster sugar
1 large egg, beaten
A little milk to blend, if necessary
1 tbsp oil, for greasing

Makes 18
Prep time: 20 mins
Cook time: 15 mins

Each cake
142 cals, 6.9g fat, 4g sat fat, 9g total sugars, 0.2g salt

V **45 mins**

1 Sift the flour, mixed spice and salt into a large bowl. Add the butter and, using your fingertips, rub in until the mixture resembles fine breadcrumbs.

2 Stir in the currants, lemon zest and 80g sugar. Add the egg and mix to a soft but firm consistency. Add a splash of milk to loosen the mixture, if necessary.

3 Roll out on a floured board to the thickness of a £1 coin. Stamp out rounds using a 5cm fluted cutter.

4 Heat a griddle or heavy-based frying pan and lightly grease with the oil. Cook the cakes, in batches, for about 3 minutes on each side, turning once. They should be dark golden and still a little soft in the centre. Dust with the remaining 20g sugar while still hot and serve straight away.

Top tip...
These simple drop scones are perfect for making with children

Hearth to heart

Back in the good old days, Welsh cakes were cooked on the hearth stone and, later, on a cast-iron griddle, or bakestone, placed over an open fire, hence the name 'bakestones' by which they are known in Wales. Unlike scones, they're not generally eaten with an accompaniment although, in the valleys in the south, they're sometimes sold ready split and spread with jam. However you prefer to eat them, a pot of good strong tea is a must.

The best of
Northern Ireland

On the menu

Northern Ireland

Giant's Causeway,
Antrim

177

Northern Ireland

Even if the humble Comber potato, Lough Neagh's eels or the Finnebrogue Estate's highly acclaimed venison don't take your fancy, there's a fantastic variety of quality meat, fish, vegetables and home-baked produce to feast on in Northern Ireland

From Londonderry to Armagh, the counties of Northern Ireland have been blessed with a mild climate, mineral-rich soil and a craggy coastline teeming with fish and seafood. As a result, Irish food culture has been shaped by centuries of farming and fishing.

The open spaces of lush countryside gave way to a rich rural tradition that still exists today. From pork to cattle, lamb, game and a wealth of vegetables, the Irish food culture is historically one of farm to fork. Today, this artisan approach has put Northern Ireland on the map for its high-quality meat, fish and cheese.

Grown here since the late 16th century, potatoes feature heavily in Irish cooking, but this beautiful land has far more going for it than just the humble spud. Traditional fare includes Irish stew, champ, soda bread, smoked fish, Finnebrogue venison, oysters and lobsters. Lough Neagh, the largest lake in Britain and Ireland, is home to Europe's biggest commercial wild eel fishery. Then there's Bushmills Irish whiskey – sure to have you dancing the jig as never before. The eating-out scene is vibrant too, with fantastic restaurants to be found in Belfast and Derry. Northern Ireland really is the place to go for the *craic* and second-to-none artisanal food.

5 foods the area is famous for

Comber potatoes Sweet and nutty, these unique new-season spuds are awaiting EU Protected Designation of Origin.

Boxty Eating this starchy potato bread was said to enhance a girl's marriage prospects: *'Boxty on the griddle, boxty in the pan. If you don't eat your boxty, you'll never get a man!'*

The Ulster fry Bacon and eggs with a Northern Irish twist.

Buttermilk This by-product of churning butter gives soda farl, pancakes and potato bread their distinctive flavours and textures.

Sausages Beef outsells the pork variety in Northern Ireland.

Did you know?

Northern Ireland has a long history of distillation – as long ago as 1276 an early settler fortified his troops with 'a mighty drop of aqua vitae'. **Bushmills Irish Whiskey** is made in Antrim at Ireland's oldest working distillery, established in 1784. Prohibition in the US dealt the Irish whiskey industry a huge blow, but Bushmills rode out the storm and today the distillery is depicted on the back of a series of banknotes.

The champs of champ

Martin and Tracy Hamilton had been successfully producing vegetables for more than 20 years, when one evening in 2003 Martin confided in a friend, over a glass of the finest Irish whiskey, that he'd love to set up a production facility on his 900-acre farm to produce champ. Within a year, a small factory had been built and Mash Direct was founded. Almost eight years on, the award-winning company, which has been supplying Sainsbury's since 2005, leads the market, making quick-serve mashed potato, vegetable and cabbage products.

Martin, a fifth generation son of the soil, says he and Tracy decided to return to the traditional tastes their mothers and grandmothers used to know. 'There are no artificial additives, preservatives or colourings in our products – just the taste and texture of homemade food.' All the Hamiltons' products are grown, steam-cooked and packaged on the farm. 'Families often have multiple earners, leaving less time for food preparation,' says Martin. 'Five a day has driven a move towards healthier prepared options.' And that can't be a bad thing.

Hillsborough International Oyster Festival

Each September, the historic village of Hillsborough, in County Down, puts on its party hat to celebrate the moreish mollusc. The festival is now in its 20th year, and still looking for a contender to better local man Colin Shirlow's 2005 Guinness World Record of eating 233 oysters in just three minutes. That's 13 every 10 seconds – gulp!

Soda bread

For bread in a hurry, this recipe is ideal – it requires minimal mixing and there's no need to knead. Fantastic served warm with lashings of butter, it'll be gone in minutes

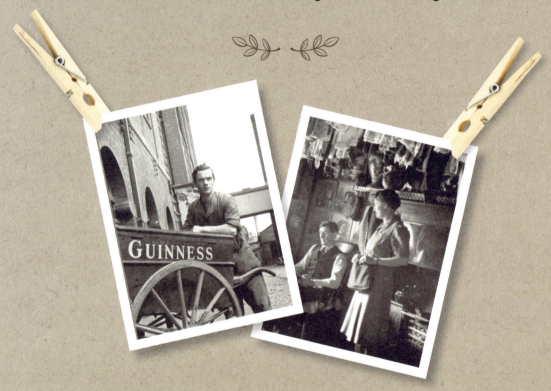

One slice or two?

Soda bread, a Northern Irish speciality, is delicious spread with butter or fried until golden as part of the famous Ulster fry.

This homely recipe developed for two reasons. Firstly, because Ireland's climate is never too warm or too cold, hard wheat varieties do not prosper, but soft wheats do. Hard wheat is ground into strong or bread flour, which needs yeast to make it rise, whereas soft wheat, being more finely milled to make plain or cake flour, rises without. Secondly, as firewood, turf and heather were abundant, any housewife with a hearthstone could bake her own bread at home rather than needing to use the village oven to conserve fuel.

There are several things that make soda bread unique, among them the inclusion of buttermilk and the cross scored into the top before baking to allow the bread to expand. In some recipes, the buttermilk is replaced by yogurt or even Guinness. Hearty stuff!

250g plain flour, plus extra for dusting
250g wholemeal plain flour
1 tsp salt
1 tsp bicarbonate of soda
1 tsp cream of tartar
1 tsp caster sugar
25g unsalted butter, diced
300ml cultured buttermilk
75–100ml semi-skimmed milk

Makes 1 loaf (8 slices)
Prep time: 20 mins
Cook time: 50 mins
....

Per slice
280 cals, 3.9g fat, 2g sat fat,
5.7g total sugars, 1.1g salt

1 Preheat the oven to 190ºC, fan 170ºC, gas 5.

2 Place all the flour, salt, bicarbonate of soda, cream of tartar and sugar in a bowl. Using your fingertips, rub in the butter until the mixture resembles breadcrumbs.

3 Stir in the buttermilk and enough milk – start with 75ml – to mix to a stiff consistency, taking care not to over-mix. Knead very lightly, then shape into a ball and flatten slightly.

4 Place the dough on a lightly floured baking tray. Cut a cross about 1.5cm deep on the top of the dough in the centre and bake for 45–50 minutes, until the loaf has risen and is golden, and the centre of the cross feels firm. Remove from the oven and wrap in a clean tea towel to cool. Best eaten on the day of making, this will also be good toasted the day after. Great served with butter.

Scallop & mushroom pie

Scallops and mushrooms work beautifully together in this pie, and the addition of sherry gives it a lovely warming flavour

1kg Maris Piper potatoes, peeled and roughly chopped
200ml semi-skimmed milk
75g slightly salted butter, plus extra for greasing
150g button mushrooms, sliced
6 spring onions, sliced
1 bay leaf
1 tbsp plain flour
4 tbsp medium sherry
500g shelled scallops, defrosted if frozen, large ones halved across the grain

Serves 4
Prep time: 20 mins
Cook time: 45 mins
....
Per serving
544 cals, 19.4g fat, 10.9g sat fat, 6.7g total sugars, 1g salt

1 Preheat the oven to 200°C, fan 180°C, gas 6. Use a little butter to grease 4 x 500ml ovenproof dishes.

2 Place the potatoes in a pan of cold water. Bring to the boil, then simmer for 10-15 minutes, until tender. Drain and mash with 25ml milk and 25g butter until smooth and creamy.

3 Meanwhile, melt 30g butter in a large pan, then add the mushrooms, spring onions and bay leaf, and fry until soft and golden. Stir in the flour and cook for 1 minute.

4 Pour in the sherry, then gradually add the remaining 175ml milk, stirring until smooth. Season with salt and freshly ground black pepper. Add the scallops and cook for 3 minutes. Remove from the heat, take out the bay leaf and spoon into the dishes.

5 Top the scallop mixture with the mashed potato and rough up the surface with a fork. Dot with the remaining 20g butter and sprinkle with freshly ground black pepper. Place on a baking tray and cook for 30 minutes, until golden.

To drink...
A refreshing unoaked chardonnay is perfect with this dish

A shore thing

Meaty yet tender, with a subtle flavour, scallops are a popular delicacy in Northern Ireland, whose coastal waters and sea loughs have long been a plentiful source. The name scallop, derived from the French *escalope*, means 'shell', and it's in the bivalve's distinctive shell that this pie is traditionally served. Scallops go well with hearty flavours such as bacon, chorizo and black pudding, and can be sautéed in butter, skewered and barbecued or used in a stir-fry.

Spanning the River Lagan,
Queen's Bridge, in Belfast,
was officially opened by
Queen Victoria in 1849

'Ireland, Sir, is like no other place under heaven, and no man can touch its sod or breathe its air without becoming better or worse'

George Bernard Shaw

Beef & stout pie

Beef and stout are perfectly paired in this succulent pie – an authentic taste of Northern Ireland that's wonderfully comforting on a cold winter's night

700g extra-lean braising steak, cut into 3cm cubes
2 tbsp plain flour
1 tbsp olive oil
1 onion, sliced
2 carrots, peeled and diced
500ml stout
300g closed-cup white mushrooms, sliced
2 cloves garlic, crushed
200ml hot beef stock
½ x 15g pack Sainsbury's fresh thyme, leaves picked
1 bay leaf
1 tbsp redcurrant jelly
375g ready-rolled puff pastry
1 medium egg, beaten

Serves 4
Prep time: 20 mins
Cook time: 2 hours, 55 mins

Per serving
774 cals, 32.5g fat, 14.4g sat fat, 14.6g total sugars, 0.6g salt

1 of 5 A-DAY

1 In a large bowl, toss the steak in the flour. Heat the oil in a large pan, then add the steak and cook, in batches, until golden all over. Remove with a slotted spoon and set aside.

2 Add the onion, carrots and 200ml stout and stir, scraping off any bits stuck to the bottom of the pan. Cook for 10 minutes, until the onion and carrot is starting to soften. Add the mushrooms and garlic, and cook for a further 2 minutes.

3 Return the meat to the pan, along with any juices, and add the stock, thyme, bay leaf and remaining 300ml stout. Bring to the boil, then cover with a lid and simmer for 2 hours over a low heat. At the end of cooking, stir in the redcurrant jelly, remove the bay leaf and divide the mixture between 4 x 250ml pie dishes.

4 Preheat the oven to 200ºC, fan 180ºC, gas 6. Cut out 4 lids from the pastry, large enough to fit over the pie dishes. Brush the edges of the dishes with some of the egg, then place the lids on top, pressing down with a fork to secure. Decorate with leaves made from pastry trimmings. Brush with egg and bake for 20-30 minutes, until golden.

Dark, rich stout — of which
Guinness is the most famous — is
the traditional drink of Ireland

Fluffy mash with spring onions — sometimes the simplest food is best

Champp

This hearty side of buttery mashed potatoes flavoured with chopped spring onions is one of Northern Ireland's most popular dishes – and it's not hard to see why

1kg Maris Piper potatoes, peeled and cut into chunks
50ml semi-skimmed milk
25g unsalted butter
1 bunch spring onions, finely chopped

Serves 6
Prep time: 10 mins
Cook time: 15 mins

Per serving
165 cals, 3.8g fat,
2.3g sat fat, 2g total
sugars, trace salt

1 Place the potatoes in a large pan of cold water. Bring to the boil, then simmer for 12-15 minutes, until tender.

2 Drain the potatoes well and return to the pan for 30 seconds to dry out, then mash with the milk and butter until smooth and fluffy.

3 Stir the spring onions through the mash, season with freshly ground black pepper and serve immediately.

Top tip...
Perfect with fried eggs and bacon, or smoked salmon and cream cheese

Potato farls

Peel 500g floury potatoes and cut into 1.5cm cubes. Steam for 15 minutes, until tender. Tip into a clean, dry pan and heat until completely dried out. Season and mash. Slowly mix in 130ml semi-skimmed milk to make a mash that just drops off the spoon. Mix in 100g plain flour, then, on a floured surface, roll into 4 rounds about 1cm thick. Heat a lightly oiled griddle pan and cook for 1-2 minutes on each side, until just starting to colour. Cut each farl into quarters and serve warm.

Serves 8 (2 quarters each)
Prep time: 15 mins
Cook time: 30 mins

Per serving 114 cals, 1.9g fat, 0.4g sat fat, 1.4g total sugars, trace salt

Top tip...
Barm brack also makes a delicious bread and butter pudding

Barm brack

Traditionally served at Halloween, this fruity bread is best enjoyed with a generous helping of butter

500g mixed dried fruit
125ml hot, strong black tea
500g strong plain flour, plus extra for dusting
75g unsalted butter, diced
½ tsp salt
1½ tsp ground mixed spice
75g sugar
1 x 7g sachet fast-action dried yeast
2 medium eggs, beaten
150–170ml semi-skimmed milk, lukewarm
Oil, for greasing

Makes 1 loaf (10 slices)
Prep time: 20 mins, plus soaking and proving time
Cook time: 50 mins

Per slice
441 cals, 8.6g fat, 4.8g sat fat, 43.2g total sugars, 0.3g salt

1 Soak the fruit in the tea for at least 2 hours.

2 Place the flour in a large mixing bowl. Using your fingertips, rub in the butter until the mixture resembles breadcrumbs. Stir in the salt, mixed spice, caster sugar and yeast.

3 Make a well in the centre of the dry ingredients, add half the beaten egg and gradually add 150ml milk, adding a little more if needed, until a slightly sticky dough is made. Turn out onto a floured surface, adding more flour if it sticks, and knead for 8–10 minutes, until the dough is elastic and smooth.

4 Add the fruit and tea and knead well until combined, sprinkling in some more flour if the dough is too wet to knead. It should be smooth but still a little sticky.

5 Place in a clean, lightly oiled bowl, cover with oiled clingfilm and leave in a warm place until doubled in size (about 1½ hours).

6 Preheat the oven to 200°C, fan 180°C, gas 6. Knead the dough lightly and shape into a ball. Place on an oiled baking tray. Brush the top with the remaining beaten egg and bake in the oven for 45–50 minutes, until golden, covering with foil if it browns too quickly. The bread should sound hollow when tapped on the base. Remove from the tin to cool.

Frightfully fruity

Barm brack is traditionally baked for Halloween, and lucky charms are sometimes wrapped up and baked into it – if you find a ring, it means you'll be getting married, a coin indicates wealth and a thimble symbolises spinsterhood. The Halloween Jack-o'-lantern also comes from an Irish folk tale. Legend has it that an Irishman called Jack played tricks on the Devil. When Jack died, the Devil wouldn't allow him into hell, so he was forced to walk the earth. The Devil, taking pity on Jack, gave him a piece of coal to light his way, and Jack put it inside a hollowed-out turnip – and so the jack-o'-lantern carved out its place in Irish folklore.

The best of
Scotland

Scotland

Argyll, Scottish Highlands

Scotland

Famed for its awe-inspiring beauty, the Scottish landscape also provides the perfect conditions for an abundance of top-quality food and drink. Add to this an array of fabulous traditional recipes and it's easy to see why Scotland is so proud of its food heritage

The food of Scotland is almost as famous as its tartan. From oysters and smoked salmon to Aberdeen Angus steak and haggis, knocked back with a wee dram of the finest single-malt whisky, Scotland's food is as wonderful as its breathtaking scenery.

Edinburgh and Glasgow have a respected food culture, with everything from farmers' markets to fine-dining restaurants all showcasing Scotland's larder, and Aberdeenshire has a long tradition of farming and fishing. As you head further north, the unspoilt environment creates the ideal conditions for superb-quality produce, including meat and game reared in the mountains and glens. The region of Speyside is famed for its malt whisky, hosting more than half of Scotland's distilleries. Head over to the Isle of Skye and, as well as a stunning landscape, you'll find spectacular local food – the island is also home to the Talisker whisky distillery and a Michelin star restaurant. With its lochs and surrounding sea, the Highlands are renowned for a wealth of seafood, delicious freshly cooked or smoked to make classic Arbroath smokies, herring, kippers and smoked salmon. If Nessie's really out there, she certainly knows how to dine in style.

The Scots also have the magic touch when it comes to cheese, with cows', sheep and goats' cheese all produced here. Cereals thrive in Scotland, especially barley, wheat and oats, and Scottish raspberries are renowned for their flavour.

And then, of course, there's Scotch whisky, or the 'water of life' as it's also known – probably Scotland's most famous export. The Scots make whisky like no other, and there is a great diversity of styles, ranging from delicate to rich to smoky. If straight up isn't quite your thing, try a drop of the good stuff in anything from porridge to cranachan. *Slàinte!*

5 foods the area is famous for

Tablet This Scottish confection, made from sugar and milk or cream, resembles crisp fudge.

Scotch beef Aberdeen Angus is famous for its tenderness and flavour, while the Highland breed is known for its marbling and succulence.

Haggis Regarded as Scotland's national dish, haggis is made from sheep's offal, oatmeal and suet – a must on Burns Night.

Arbroath smokie Whole, wood-smoked haddock with a luscious savoury flavour that ordinary smoked haddock just cannot match.

Salmon Wild and farmed salmon is vitally important to the economy of Scotland's West Highlands and islands, and the region is particularly renowned for its smoked salmon.

Did you know?

Just like wine, honey varies in appearance and taste depending on the area it comes from. Scottish heather honey is sourced from hives of bees that forage on wild heather, diligently harvesting its nectar and pollen. With its darker amber colour and distinctive tangy, slightly smoky taste, no wonder there's such a buzz about it.

Going with the flow

The team at Marine Harvest's Greshornish fish farm – including assistant site manager Calum Nicolson (pictured), who has been with the company for more than 20 years – works in and around Scotland's Outer Hebrides to meet customer demand for responsibly sourced salmon with superb taste and texture.

Marine Harvest has been farming salmon since 1971 and supplies Sainsbury's with fresh fish from their 30 sea farms. All the fish are reared and harvested in compliance with the RSPCA Freedom Foods scheme. Remotely located on a sea loch at the north end of Skye, nearly 30 miles from the next fish farm, Greshornish houses 12 underwater pens.

'I'm lucky enough to have a job I really enjoy,' says Calum. 'It involves a wide range of tasks, from engineering and IT to animal husbandry, and as this is a young industry, we're learning all the time. Working at Greshornish has enabled me to work on my native island and I enjoy the beautiful scenery and abundant wildlife that surrounds us every day.'

Castle Douglas – foodie heaven

Stroll along the charming streets of the historic market town of Castle Douglas in Dumfries & Galloway, and you'll stumble across more than 50 shops offering local food and drink. This designated food town also hosts a calendar of events, such as food fairs and chefs' masterclasses.

Traditional porridge

A bowl of steaming hot porridge makes a brilliant start to the day. The ultimate comfort food on a cold winter's morning, it provides you with energy and tastes heavenly, too. No wonder this Scottish institution is now loved the world over

Know your oats

Porridge has been a staple of the Scottish diet for generations, largely because oats grow so well in the country's wet, cool conditions. Served with lashings of milk, porridge was affordable, a source of protein and not just for breakfast – hot, salty porridge was also poured into a mould and left to set, then sliced and given to workers for their midday meal, as it was easier to carry than brittle oatcakes. To this day, many Scots agree that there's no place in a bowl of porridge for sugar, honey or any other sweet additions. Other traditions that are alive and well include stirring the porridge during cooking with a special stick known as a spurtle, and eating the finished product with a horn-handled spoon. Every October the World Porridge Making Championship is fiercely contested in the Highland village of Carrbridge (above right), where the porridge is judged on consistency, taste and colour. The prize? A golden spurtle, of course.

200g Scottish porridge oats
1.2 litres water or milk, or a
mixture of both
½ tsp salt

Serves 4
Cook time: 10 mins

Per serving
251 cals, 6.6g fat, 2.2g sat fat,
8.1g total sugars, 0.8g salt

1 Place all the ingredients in a large saucepan. Bring to a gentle boil, stirring continuously until the porridge begins to thicken.

2 After about 5 minutes, when the porridge has thickened and the oats are cooked, remove from the heat and allow to stand for a minute before serving.

Scotch broth

This hearty, warming soup is one of Scotland's most famous dishes and, served with fresh, crusty bread, is a meal in itself

300g boned lamb shoulder or lamb neck fillet, trimmed and cubed, or beef, cubed
2 litres lamb or chicken stock
80g Sainsbury's dried country soup mix
1 medium leek, washed and finely diced
1 onion, finely diced
2 medium carrots, peeled and finely diced
2 sticks celery, finely diced
¼ small swede, finely diced
¼ savoy cabbage, finely shredded

Serves 6
Prep time: 20 mins
Cook time: 1½ hours

Per serving
207 cals, 7.8g fat,
3.1g sat fat, 7.8g total
sugars, trace salt

2.5 A-DAY

1 Place the lamb or beef in a large pan and cover with the stock. Season with freshly ground black pepper, then add the country soup mix. Bring to the boil and simmer for 1 hour, until tender.

2 Add the leek, onion, carrots, celery and swede, and simmer for another 20 minutes. Add the cabbage and simmer for 3-4 minutes, then season with salt and freshly ground black pepper to taste. Great served with plenty of crusty bread.

Souper bowl

There's some disagreement as to whether Scotch broth, also known as hotch-potch, should be made with lamb or beef. Some early recipes even used fowl as the boiled meat. Vegetables were fairly interchangeable too – from carrots and swedes to leeks and even marigolds – but the inclusion of barley appears to be non-negotiable. The meat was occasionally removed from the pot and served separately, but these days it's all dished up together. It was served to Dr Johnson, the distinguished man of letters, when he visited the Highlands in the 18th century. Apparently he was rather taken with it, and ate several bowls.

Haggis with neeps 'n' tatties

This tasty combination of mashed spuds and swede is the perfect foil for many meat dishes – including the all-important haggis, of course. A match made in Highland heaven

Burns Night bash

Every January 25, Scots around the world hold parties and dinners to celebrate the birth date of their national poet, Robert Burns, fondly known as Rabbie. Born in 1759, Burns was passionate about freedom and equality, and as famous for his *joie de vivre* as his liking for the 'lassies'. He was a great wordsmith and his poem *Auld Lang Syne*, set to a folk tune, remains unrivalled as the song sung at midnight as the bells sound the New Year. Essential ingredients for a good Burns Night supper include music, dancing, recitals of Burns' poems and fine Scottish fare such as cock-a-leekie soup, neeps 'n' tatties, cranachan and, of course, haggis, that much-loved national icon, which Burns called 'the great chieftain of the puddin'-race'. It's customary for the haggis to be piped in by bagpipers dressed in the full regalia of tartan kilt and sporran. Add a few wee drams of whisky into the mix and you'll have a Burns Night to be proud of.

450g haggis
700g swede, peeled and cubed
500g Maris Piper potatoes, peeled and cubed
40g salted butter
Grating of nutmeg (optional)
1 dram of whisky (optional)

Serves 4
Prep time: 10 mins
Cook time: 45-90 mins
(depending on cook time for the haggis)

....

Per serving
576 cals, 33.4g fat, 14.4g sat fat, 9.5g total sugars, 2.4g salt

1 Cook the haggis following pack instructions.

2 Meanwhile, place the swede and potatoes in separate saucepans, and cover each with cold water. Bring to the boil and cook for 15-20 minutes, until tender.

3 Drain and place over a low heat to dry them out completely.

4 Add 20g butter to each pan and mash together with the swede and potatoes respectively, grating over some nutmeg, if using. Season with salt and freshly ground black pepper. Serve with the haggis doused in the whisky, if desired.

Cullen skink

Chowder with a Scottish twist, Cullen skink is a quick, easy dish that's packed full of flavour and makes a hearty family meal

400g undyed smoked haddock fillets
1 onion, chopped
3 large potatoes, peeled and chopped
2 dried bay leaves
450ml whole milk
1 tbsp chopped fresh flat-leaf parsley
Oatcakes, to serve

Serves 4
Prep time: 15 mins
Cook time: 30 mins

....

Per serving
436 cals, 9.4g fat, 4.1g sat fat, 9.6g total sugars, 2g salt

1 Pour 750ml cold water into a large saucepan and add the haddock, making sure it's covered by the water. Bring to a simmer and cook for 3-4 minutes, being careful not to overcook the fish. Remove the haddock from the pan and set aside.

2 Add the onion, potatoes and bay leaves to the water in the pan. Season well with freshly ground black pepper and simmer for 15 minutes, until the vegetables are tender.

3 Meanwhile, gently flake the fish, removing any bones and skin.

4 Remove the bay leaves from the pan and gently mash together the potatoes and onion, just enough to break them up slightly. Add the milk.

5 Return the fish to the pan and add the parsley. Bring to a gentle simmer and season with freshly ground black pepper. Serve in bowls, with oatcakes on the side. Great with a swirl of cream for extra richness.

Top tip...
Add a 198g tin of drained sweetcorn with the parsley for an alternative flavour

Where's the catch?

The name Cullen skink may sound odd, but it does make perfect sense. In the 1890s, in the northeastern fishing town of Cullen, locals coped with a shortage of meat by making their usual 'skink' soup with readily available smoked haddock instead of the traditional beef shins that gave the dish its name. The resulting soup, which is similar to chowder, is now popular right across the land - not bad going, considering its humble beginnings.

Game pie

Scotland has a rich history of wild game, and this fusion of pheasant, rabbit and venison is perfection wrapped in pastry

200g pheasant breast, cut into 2–3cm pieces

340g venison fillet, cut into 2–3cm pieces

1 x 300g pack Taste the Difference diced wild rabbit, cut into 2–3cm pieces

2½ tbsp sunflower oil

2 carrots, peeled and roughly chopped

1 onion, roughly chopped

2 sticks celery, roughly chopped

2 cloves garlic, finely chopped

1½ tbsp plain flour, plus extra for dusting

300ml red wine

½ x 15g pack Sainsbury's fresh thyme, torn into sprigs

600ml hot chicken stock

1 large egg, beaten, for glazing

1 x 500g block Sainsbury's shortcrust pastry

Serves 8
Prep time: 35 mins, plus cooling time
Cook time: 3 hours

....

Per serving
559 cals, 30.8g fat, 14.6g sat fat, 5.1g total sugars, 0.9g salt

1 Season all the meat with salt and freshly ground black pepper. Heat ½ tbsp oil in a large, heavy-bottomed, flameproof lidded casserole dish over a medium heat. Add the pheasant and cook for 5-10 minutes, until browned. Remove from the pan and allow to cool, then place in the fridge. Add 1 tbsp oil to the casserole dish and fry the venison and rabbit in batches, for 5-10 minutes, until golden all over. Set aside.

2 Reduce the heat, then add the remaining 1 tbsp oil and all the vegetables to the casserole dish and fry for 5 minutes. Add the garlic and flour, and fry for a further 30 seconds. Pour in the wine and cook until reduced by half, then return the venison and rabbit to the casserole dish, along with the thyme. Pour in the stock, bring to the boil, cover and cook for 1¼ hours. Remove the lid and cook for a further 15 minutes, until the sauce has thickened and the meat is tender. Stir in the pheasant, then allow to cool before removing the thyme stalks.

3 Preheat the oven to 200°C, fan 180°C, gas 6. Transfer the contents of the casserole dish into a 1.5-litre pie dish and brush the edges of the dish with a little beaten egg.

4 On a floured surface, roll out the pastry to a circle slightly bigger than the top of the pie dish and to the thickness of a £1 coin, then cut 2 long strips from the excess and press them around the rim of the dish. Brush them with egg, then top with the pastry lid. Trim the edges, press to seal and cut a slit for steam to escape. Decorate with leaves made from pastry trimmings. Brush the pastry with the remaining beaten egg and bake for 50 minutes, until golden. Great with mashed potatoes and green beans.

The view over Edinburgh from Calton Hill, with the monument to Scottish philosopher Dugald Stewart in the foreground

'We look to Scotland for all our ideas of civilisation'

Voltaire

Cock-a-leekie soup

Traditionally served on Burns Night, this warming combination of chicken and leeks makes one of the loveliest ladlefuls around

1.35kg Sainsbury's whole chicken
1 onion, roughly chopped
2 carrots, peeled and roughly chopped
2 sticks celery, roughly chopped
2 bay leaves
10 peppercorns
100g ready-to-eat pitted prunes, sliced
1 x 500g pack Sainsbury's extra trimmed leeks, sliced
½ x 28g pack Sainsbury's fresh flat-leaf parsley, chopped

Serves 6
Prep time: 20 mins
Cook time: 2 hours, 10 mins

Per serving
193 cals, 3.3g fat, 0.9g sat fat, 7.5g total sugars, 0.3g salt

1 Place the chicken in a snug-fitting lidded saucepan with the onion, carrots, celery, bay leaves and peppercorns.

2 Cover with about 3 litres cold water and gently bring to a simmer, then cover and cook for 1¼ hours to make a stock.

3 Remove the chicken from the stock and set aside.

4 Strain the stock into a clean saucepan, discarding the vegetables, bay leaves and peppercorns. Add the prunes and leeks to the pan, then cover and cook for a further 45 minutes.

5 Meanwhile, strip the chicken from the bones and shred roughly, then add back into the soup. Season with salt and freshly ground black pepper and warm through. Serve sprinkled with the parsley.

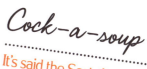

Cock-a-soup

It's said the Scots have been fuelled by cock-a-leekie soup since medieval times – though the name is believed to have been coined in the 18th century. It was originally served as two courses, with the chicken and the broth eaten separately. These days, some people prefer to remove the prunes before serving, or even leave them out of the recipe completely, but their texture, flavour and colour give this dish its uniqueness. Simple and wholesome, cock-a-leekie is a staple of Burns Night celebrations on January 25 (see page 200), when it is usually served as a starter before the main event of haggis.

Whether chewy or crunchy,
flapjacks are hard to beat

Flapjacks

These heart-warming treats are as buttery as they come and pack a scrumptiously oaty punch

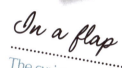

200g slightly salted butter, roughly chopped, plus extra for greasing
75g demerara sugar
6 tbsp golden syrup
100g Taste the Difference whole rolled porridge oats
250g Scottish porridge oats

Makes 9
Prep time: 5 mins
Cook time: 30 mins

···

Per flapjack
382 cals, 21.6g fat, 11.8g sat fat, 19.4g total sugars, 0.5g salt

V **45 mins**

1 Preheat the oven to 180ºC, fan 160ºC, gas 4. Grease a 20cm square baking tin and line with baking parchment.

2 Melt the butter, sugar and golden syrup together in a large saucepan, then simmer for 30 seconds. Remove from the heat.

3 Mix in both types of oats, then transfer the mixture to the baking tin and press down with the back of a spoon.

4 Bake for 20 minutes, until golden, for chewy flapjacks or 25 minutes for crunchy ones. Cut into 9 squares while still hot and leave to cool in the tray.

In a flap

The curious name 'flapjack' is first recorded in the early 17th century, but it probably referred to a flat tart or pancake. It's been suggested these pancakes got their name because of the custom to 'flap' (or 'flip') them in the pan – indeed, in America, pancakes are still known as flapjacks. The oaty flapjacks we love today didn't appear until the 20th century.

Ecclefechan tarts

Deep cups of buttery pastry filled with plump vine fruits, Ecclefechan tarts are Scotland's mouthwatering answer to the mince pie

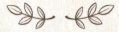

150g plain flour, plus extra for dusting
60g unsalted cold butter, cubed
25g caster sugar
1 medium egg yolk
70g unsalted butter, melted
and cooled
100g light brown soft sugar
1 medium egg, beaten
1 tsp white wine vinegar
30g walnuts, chopped
150g mixed dried fruit
30g glacé cherries, chopped

Makes 12
Prep time: 20 mins,
plus chilling time
Cook time: 15 mins

Per tart
242 cals, 11.8g fat, 6.3g sat fat,
20.6g total sugars, trace salt

V

1 To make the pastry, place the flour in a large bowl and, using your fingertips, rub in the cubed butter until the mixture resembles fine breadcrumbs. Stir in the caster sugar. Add the egg yolk and enough cold water (about 1 tbsp) to mix to a firm dough. Wrap in clingfilm, then place in the fridge to chill for 15 minutes.

2 Preheat the oven to 190ºC, fan 170ºC, gas 5. On a lightly floured surface, roll out the pastry to the thickness of a £1 coin. Using a round cutter, stamp out 12 rounds and use to line a 12-hole tart tin. Prick the pastry cases with a fork.

3 Place all the remaining ingredients in a large bowl. Mix together, then spoon into the tart cases. Bake for about 15 minutes, until the pastry is golden and the filling has set.

Try this...
Delicious served
warm with
a dollop of
brandy butter

Break for the border

Reminiscent, with its caramel-like filling, of pecan pie, this style of tart is a speciality of the Borders, a region stretching from the English border to just south of Edinburgh. Many variations exist, hence its common name, 'border tart'. This fruity version is named after the town of Ecclefechan in Dumfries & Galloway, birthplace of the satirist Thomas Carlyle (pictured). It makes a great alternative to mince pie, but is too good to keep just for Christmas!

Top tip...
Instead of whisky,
drizzle over
a little Drambuie
or Glayva

Cranachan

Deliciously creamy and fruity with mellow honey and whisky flavours, cranachan is the ultimate Scottish dessert

50g pinhead oatmeal (available in Sainsbury's Special Selection) or medium oatmeal (such as Mornflake)
1 x 600ml pot Sainsbury's double cream
4 tbsp Scotch whisky
3 tbsp Taste the Difference Scottish heather honey, plus extra for serving
2 x 170g punnets fresh raspberries

Serves 6
Prep time: 10 mins
Cook time: 3–4 mins

Per serving
533 cals, 48.4g fat, 29.7g sat fat, 13.7g total sugars, trace salt

(V) (45 mins)

1 Preheat the grill. Spread the oatmeal out in an even layer on a baking tray and grill until toasted, watching it carefully so it doesn't burn.

2 Pour the cream into a large bowl and lightly whip until it is just starting to hold its shape. Gently stir through the whisky, honey and two-thirds of the toasted oatmeal.

3 Spoon half the cream mixture into 6 x 200ml glasses, top with half the raspberries, then spoon over the remaining cream mixture. Sprinkle over the remaining oatmeal and raspberries, and drizzle with honey before serving.

Cream of the crop

Perhaps the most famous Scottish dessert, cranachan was traditionally consumed around harvest time. Back then, the ingredients were brought to the table in separate dishes and diners assembled the pudding according to their own taste. Many Scots call it 'crowdie cream' because a soft local cheese called crowdie was once included in the recipe. Cranachan still makes use of great regional ingredients – Scottish raspberries are renowned for their flavour and heather honey has a distinctive taste and scent. For a 'virgin' cranachan that kids can enjoy, swap the whisky for a few drops of vanilla essence.

Dundee cake

This rich, fruity cake, with a whole-almond topping, is every bit as popular today as when it was invented in the 19th-century

150g unsalted butter, softened, plus extra for greasing
150g caster sugar
3 large eggs
225g plain flour, sifted
1 tsp baking powder
2 tbsp semi-skimmed milk
175g sultanas
175g raisins
75g glacé cherries, halved
50g cut mixed peel
30g ground almonds
Zest of 1 large orange
50g whole blanched almonds

Serves 12
Prep time: 20 mins
Cook time: 1½ hours

Per serving
402 cals, 16.6g fat, 7.9g sat fat, 40.1g total sugars, 0.2g salt

1 Preheat the oven to 180°C, fan 160°C, gas 4. Lightly butter a deep 19cm cake tin and line with baking parchment.

2 Place the butter and sugar in a large bowl, and beat with an electric whisk until light and fluffy. Gradually add the eggs, one at a time, beating well after each addition. Fold in the flour, baking powder and milk, then the sultanas, raisins, cherries, mixed peel, ground almonds and orange zest.

3 Spoon the mixture into the prepared cake tin and smooth the surface. Gently arrange the whole almonds in neat rings on top of the cake.

4 Place on a baking tray and bake in the centre of the oven for 1¼-1½ hours. The cake is ready when a skewer inserted into the centre comes out clean and the top is golden.

5 Leave to cool in the tin, then cut into slices to serve.

Nuts about cake

Dundee has been known for its marmalade since the late 1700s, and this fruitcake, with its distinctive topping of whole almonds, was created as a by-product of the marmalade industry. Keiller's, the city's famous marmalade-makers, began baking the cake when Seville oranges were out of season, thus cannily ensuring that factory workers were kept busy year round and that leftover peel did not go to waste. Rich and fruity, Dundee cake makes a great alternative to Christmas cake.

Scottish shortbread

Perfected over centuries, classic Scottish shortbread is sweet and buttery, simple and satisfying – and moreishly melt-in-the-mouth. No wonder it's long been a favourite with queens and biscuit-lovers alike

Take the biscuit

Shortbread is a Scottish speciality, although similar recipes, such as that for Shrewsbury cakes, do crop up elsewhere. Petticoat tails are crumbly shortbread biscuits baked in a round and then broken into triangular segments. Their unusual name may be a corruption of *petites galettes* - the French cakes loved by Mary, Queen of Scots (above left), who spent most of her youth in France and brought them to Scotland in the mid-1500s. It is also possible the biscuits were named for their resemblance to the hooped crinoline petticoats worn by the ladies of Mary's court. Whichever is true, they are certainly fit for a queen. The classic shortbread recipe is given here, but there are many variations. The thick Pitcaithly bannock is made with peel and almonds, while the recipe made for Queen Victoria (above right) when she was at Balmoral was seasoned with salt, and the Ayrshire version contains egg yolk and cream for extra richness.

200g plain flour
50g ground rice
80g caster sugar, plus extra
for sprinkling
150g unsalted butter, at room
temperature

Makes 10
Prep time: 15 mins
Cook time: 50 mins
....
Each shortbread
239 cals, 12.5g fat, 8.1g sat fat,
9.8g total sugars, trace salt

1 Preheat the oven to 150ºC, fan 130ºC, gas 2. Place the flour, ground rice and sugar in a large bowl and mix together. Using your fingertips, rub in the butter. Work the mixture with your hands until it starts to bind together, taking care not to overwork the dough as it will become oily.

2 Press the mixture into the base of a 20cm round, fluted tart tin. Using the back of a spoon, gently smooth the top. Mark around the edge of the dough with a fork. Using a round 2.5-3cm metal cutter, cut a circle in the centre. Remove the cutter, leaving the dough in place. Mark the outer circle into 10 segments and prick all over with a fork.

3 Bake for 40–50 minutes, until pale straw in colour. Remove from the oven and, while still warm, cut through the sections, marking the edge again with a fork if necessary. Leave to cool in the tin. Lightly dredge with caster sugar before serving.

Great British traditions

As a nation, we Brits have always been proud of our heritage. But it's not all about castles and coats of arms. Our culinary history gives us plenty to shout about, too, with quaint and quirky traditions keeping kitchens busy all year round. So take a tip from Grandma and try some of our favourites

All foods
weird & wonderful

Britain is home to a host of unique food-related festivities that make even caber tossing and morris dancing look positively humdrum

The turning of the seasons is one of the real joys of living in Britain and, for centuries, we've marked the passing of the year with festivals and traditions that have one thing in common – a love of food. Our seasonal specialities don't stop at Christmas and Easter, so there's always an excuse to celebrate. From the simple fun of Pancake Day to the spooky goings-on at Halloween, food is prepared according to time-honoured recipes. And there are plenty more unusual food events that take place throughout the year...

The seeds of Halloween

Most people consider apple bobbing to be a convivial tradition associated with Halloween, but tell that to the health officials in Southampton who, in 2010, suggested that stalks were removed and goggles donned before the party started. For centuries, apples have been linked to autumn, when the Romans celebrated Pomona, the goddess of apple trees and fruits. When they came to Britain, the Romans held this festival on 31 October and apples became part of the harvest celebration that later became Halloween.

Say cheese

In the usually quiet Gloucestershire parish of Brockworth, grown men and women can be seen hurtling down a steep hill in pursuit of an 8lb double Gloucester in the annual Cheese Rolling contest, held every May. Injuries are fairly commonplace as the fearless competitors fight for the treasured prize. And the winner receives – yes, you guessed it – a cheese.

Quirky customs and peculiar practices are embraced with enthusiasm across the land

Hare-brained fun

Easter Monday sees the centuries-old Hare Pie Scramble and Bottle Kicking hit the Leicestershire village of Hallaton. Food flies as pieces of the pie are thrown into the wild crowd, and the men of the village show their strength, joining the scrum to battle over a keg of ale. Surely there are easier ways to get a beer!

No pain, no gain

As a nation known for its eccentricity, Britain doesn't disappoint with its edible events, but who'd have guessed that nettle-eating forms part of the culinary calendar? Annual championships take place in Dorset, with competitors plucking and eating nettles from 2ft-long stalks – the one who consumes the most in an hour is the winner. Pass the dock leaves...

Bun fight!

The Oxfordshire town of Abingdon has, for the past 250 years or so, celebrated important events by hurling fruit buns from the roof of the county hall to the waiting crowds below. More than 4,000 buns were thrown to mark the wedding of Prince William to Kate Middleton. Other bun-worthy events have included Queen Victoria's coronation, VE Day, the Millennium and the Queen Mother's 100th birthday. The Abingdon County Hall Museum houses carefully preserved buns from some of these memorable events, dating back to 1887.

Try this...
To go savoury, omit the sugar, then fill your pancakes with cheese and ham

Pancakes

We enjoy them all year round but, historically, pancakes were a naughty indulgence before a period of being very good

150g plain flour
25g caster sugar, plus extra to serve
Pinch of salt
1 medium egg, plus 1 medium yolk
350ml semi-skimmed milk
25g unsalted butter, melted
½ tsp vanilla extract
A little sunflower oil, for frying
Juice of 1 lemon, to serve

Makes 12 (serves 6)
Prep time: 10 mins, plus resting time
Cook time: 20 mins

Per serving
243 cals, 8.5g fat, 3.7g sat fat, 16.1g total sugars, 0.3g salt

V 45 mins

1 Sift the flour into a large bowl, then stir in the sugar and salt.

2 Whisk the egg, egg yolk and milk together in a jug. Make a well in the middle of the flour, then gradually beat in the milk mixture with a wooden spoon, drawing in the flour from the edges to make a batter the consistency of single cream. Stir in the melted butter and vanilla extract, and set aside for 10 minutes.

3 Brush a 20cm non-stick frying pan with sunflower oil and place over a medium heat. When the pan is hot, pour in a ladleful of batter. Swirl the pan so that the base is covered in a thin, even layer. Cook for about 1 minute, until light golden. Using a spatula, flip the pancake over and cook on the other side for a further 30 seconds, until golden. Transfer to a warm plate and repeat the process until you have 12 pancakes.

4 Serve warm, sprinkled with sugar and lemon juice.

Flippin' lovely pancakes

Pancakes were traditionally cooked the day before the start of Lent to use up ingredients, such as butter and eggs, that were not supposed to be eaten in the six-week run-up to Easter. Communities across the country celebrate the day with pancake races, the most famous one taking place in the Buckinghamshire town of Olney. The race dates back more than 500 years and is open to housewives and young women of the town, who must wear an apron and a headscarf or hat. The winner is rewarded with a kiss from the verger. Talk about racy!

Simnel cake

This marzipan-rich classic is a deliciously fruity foil to the chocolate indulgences of the Easter season

Icing sugar, to dust
1 x 454g pack Sainsbury's marzipan
250g plain flour, plus a little extra if needed
1 tsp freshly grated nutmeg
1 tsp ground cinnamon
Pinch of salt
Zest of 1 orange
100g glacé cherries, halved
50g chopped mixed peel
175g sultanas
175g raisins
125g currants
175g butter, softened, plus extra for greasing
175g golden caster sugar
4 medium eggs, lightly beaten and at room temperature
3 tbsp milk
1 tbsp apricot jam, warmed
1 medium egg, beaten, to glaze

Serves 12
Prep time: 30 mins
Cook time: 2 hours
....
Per serving
604 cals, 20.9g fat, 9.4g sat fat, 77g total sugars, 0.2g salt

1 Preheat the oven to 150ºC, fan 130ºC, gas 2. Grease a deep, 19cm round cake tin and line with a double layer of baking parchment. On a surface dusted with icing sugar, roll out 175g marzipan to a 19cm circle, about 8mm thick.

2 Sift the flour, nutmeg, cinnamon and salt into a large bowl. Stir in the zest, cherries, peel, sultanas, raisins and currants.

3 In another bowl, cream the butter and sugar until light and fluffy. Gradually beat in the eggs, adding a little extra flour if the mixture begins to curdle. Add the flour and fruit mixture, and the milk, then mix to a soft dropping consistency.

4 Spoon half the mixture into the tin, then smooth the surface and cover with the marzipan circle. Spoon over the remaining mixture and smooth again. Cover with a double layer of baking parchment and cut a small hole in the middle of the paper. Bake for 2 hours, until the top is golden and a skewer inserted into the centre comes out clean. Leave in the tin to cool, then remove from the tin.

5 Preheat the grill to a medium-high heat.

6 On a surface dusted with icing sugar, roll out more marzipan into a 19cm circle, about 8mm thick. Brush the top of the cake with some of the jam and lay the marzipan circle over the top. Using a large knife, lightly score a lattice pattern into the marzipan. Roll the leftover marzipan into 11 balls and arrange around the edge of the cake using a little jam to secure in place. Brush with the beaten egg and place under the grill for 3-4 minutes, until the marzipan starts to turn golden.

A moveable feast

Versions of the simnel cake are believed to have been made as far back as medieval times. For many years, it was associated with Mothering Sunday and was given as a present on the fourth Sunday of Lent. As it became part of Easter celebrations, the marzipan ingredient was adapted to include 11 decorative balls on the top of the cake, representing the apostles minus the traitor, Judas.

Hot cross buns

Traditionally served on Good Friday, hot cross buns remain as popular as ever. The best way to serve them? Fresh from the oven

175g mixed dried fruit
Zest of 1 orange
1 x 7g sachet fast-action dried yeast
175g caster sugar
300ml semi-skimmed milk, warmed
600g strong white bread flour
Pinch of salt
3 tsp mixed spice
½ tsp ground cinnamon
A good grating of fresh nutmeg
75g unsalted butter, softened, plus 1 tbsp melted butter
Oil, for greasing
1 egg yolk mixed with 1 tbsp milk
50g plain flour

Makes 16
Prep time: 20 mins, plus proving time
Cook time: 20 mins

Per bun
273 cals, 6g fat, 3.5g sat fat, 20.4g total sugars, 0.1g salt

1 In a bowl, mix together the dried fruit and orange zest, and set aside. Place the yeast in a jug with 15g caster sugar. Pour over 4 tbsp warm milk and allow to foam for 5 minutes.

2 Place the bread flour, salt, mixed spice, cinnamon, nutmeg, softened butter and 110g caster sugar in a food processor, and pulse until the mixture resembles breadcrumbs. Tip into a large bowl and make a well in the centre. Pour in the yeast and most of the remaining warm milk. Mix into a sticky dough, adding more milk if required. Knead for 8-10 minutes, until smooth and elastic. Knead in the dried fruit and zest, and cover with oiled clingfilm. Leave in a warm place to rise until doubled in size (about 1 hour).

3 Press the dough into a rectangular shape. Divide and shape into 16 equal balls. Place on baking trays lined with baking parchment, leaving a little space between each bun for it to rise. Cover with a clean damp tea towel and leave in a warm place until doubled in size and joined together - this may take up to 1 hour, depending on the temperature.

4 Preheat the oven to 230°C, fan 210°C, gas 8. Gently brush the buns with the egg yolk and milk mixture.

5 Mix the plain flour with the melted butter and 4 tbsp water to form a paste. Spoon into a piping bag with a small, round, plain nozzle and pipe a cross on each bun. Bake for 5 minutes, then reduce the oven temperature to 190°C, fan 170°C, gas 5 and bake for a further 10-15 minutes, until golden. Turn out onto a wire rack to cool, then gently pull the buns apart.

6 Gently heat the remaining 50g caster sugar with 2 tbsp water until dissolved. Bring to the boil, then brush over the buns. Allow to cool before serving.

One a penny, two a penny...

There are many superstitions associated with these fruity buns, topped with the traditional Easter cross. On Good Friday, cooks often baked a bun for so long that it dried out and they would hang it in their kitchen for the rest of the year. This 'good luck' bun was said to protect the home from fire, and it could also be grated into medicine to ward off ailments. Sounds like just what you'd need if you were feeling a bit poorly...

To drink...

Make vampire's blood: lemonade, orange and cranberry juice with a dash of blackcurrant cordial

Floating ghost muffins

Children will love baking and eating these Halloween muffins – they're dead easy to make and frightfully good fun

200g dark chocolate, broken into pieces
50ml sunflower oil
1 medium egg
200ml semi-skimmed milk
250g self-raising flour
2 tbsp cocoa powder
1 tsp bicarbonate of soda
150g light brown soft sugar
100g white chocolate, broken into pieces
1 x 500g pack Sainsbury's ready-to-roll white icing
100g apricot jam, thinned with 1 tbsp water
2 tbsp black food colouring

Makes 12
Prep time: 30 mins, plus cooling and setting time
Cook time: 25 mins

Per muffin
508 cals, 16.8g fat, 7.9g sat fat, 66.7g total sugars, 0.9g salt

Ⓥ

1 Preheat the oven to 180°C, fan 160°C, gas 4. Line a 12-hole muffin tin with paper cases.

2 Place 100g dark chocolate in a heatproof bowl and melt over a pan of simmering water. Remove and allow to cool slightly before stirring in the oil, egg and milk.

3 Place the flour, cocoa powder, bicarbonate of soda, sugar, white chocolate and remaining 100g dark chocolate in a large bowl. Stir in the chocolate mixture, taking care not to over-stir. Spoon into the cases until they are three-quarters full. Bake for 20-25 minutes, then leave to cool on a wire rack.

4 Cut the rounded top off each muffin to make a flat surface. Turn the muffins upside down on a board and gently peel off the cases.

5 Roll out the icing to a thickness of about 5mm. Using a saucer about 13cm in diameter, cut out 12 rounds, re-rolling the trimmings if necessary. Brush the tops of the muffins with the jam, then place a circle of icing over each. Press to flatten the top then make draping folds around the edges to create floating ghosts.

6 Paint on ghoulish faces with the black colouring and leave to dry for 10 minutes before serving.

Festival fare

Spooky recipes have been popular at Halloween parties in recent years, but special food to mark 31 October has older origins. It all kicked off with the pagan festival of Samhain, meaning 'summer's end'. This harvest celebration was a time for honouring the dead and seeing into the future. Apples from the harvest played an important role (read about apple bobbing on page 222) and, in some parts of the North, the festival was known as Nut Crack Night, and nuts were thrown onto the fire for fortune-telling. Trick-or-treating has its origins in the spiced buns, or soul cakes, commemorating the dead, that were given to children and the poor.

Toffee apples

Deliciously crisp and unashamedly sticky, toffee apples are a yummy treat
for all the family – perfect when watching the fireworks on Bonfire Night

Gunpowder, toffee and plot

Sticky as seaside rock and just as nostalgia-inducing, toffee apples have become a sweet tradition commonly enjoyed at Halloween and Guy Fawkes Night, because both festivals fall in the wake of the annual apple harvest. The practice of coating fruit in sugar syrup dates back to ancient times, as honey and sugar were used as preserving agents, but toffee apples are thought to date back to the late 19th century. The crunch of one of these appley treats on a crisp autumn evening while stood round a bonfire is unbeatable – and homemade ones taste so much better than shop-bought. They're easy to make and you can use your favourite eating apple for toffee apples, while mildly tart varieties, such as Braeburn, are best used for the caramel version shown here. If you wish, you can dip them in hundreds & thousands or chopped nuts before leaving them to set. Not so sure a toffee apple a day will keep the doctor away, though...

10 lolly sticks
10 Braeburn apples, scrubbed
to remove wax residue and
with stalks removed
500g light brown soft sugar
1 tbsp white wine vinegar
50g unsalted butter
3 tbsp golden syrup

Makes 10
Prep time: 15 mins,
plus setting time
Cook time: 20 mins

Per toffee apple
309 cals, 4.3g fat, 2.7g sat fat,
66g total sugars, trace salt

1 Push a lolly stick into the stalk end of each apple.

2 Place the sugar in a heavy-based pan with 120ml cold water. Heat gently, stirring until the sugar dissolves. Bring to the boil, without stirring, then add the vinegar, butter and syrup.

3 Boil for about 12 minutes, until the mixture is at the soft-crack stage – if you pour a drop into cold water, it should form threads that bend slightly before breaking. If using a sugar thermometer, the caramel is ready when the temperature reaches 138°C.

4 Carefully dip the apples in the hot caramel, turning to coat, then leave to set on a baking tray lined with baking parchment for about 15 minutes.

The crunch of these appley treats around the bonfire is unbeatable

Roast turkey

It wouldn't be Christmas without a traditional dinner. A century ago, that meant roast goose, but now turkey reigns supreme – and you can see why

125g unsalted butter, softened, plus extra for greasing

1 heaped tbsp fresh thyme leaves

1 x 20g pack Sainsbury's fresh sage, finely chopped

2 cloves garlic, finely chopped

1 x 5kg free-range turkey

1 x 220g pack Taste the Difference smoked streaky bacon rashers

For the stuffing balls

1 x 500g pack Sainsbury's Butcher's Choice pork sausagemeat

45g fresh white breadcrumbs

140g chestnuts, cooked, peeled and chopped

20g fresh flat-leaf parsley, finely chopped

1 onion, finely chopped

Zest of ½ lemon

¼ tsp ground cloves

1 medium egg, beaten

Serves 10
Prep time: 45 mins
Cook time: 4 hours, plus resting time

Per serving
532 cals, 34.7g fat, 15.9g sat fat, 2g total sugars, 1.6g salt

1 Preheat the oven to 200ºC, fan 180ºC, gas 6. In a bowl, mix together the butter, thyme, sage and garlic, and season to taste with salt and freshly ground black pepper.

2 Being careful not to tear the skin, use your fingertips to separate the turkey skin from the breast meat. Push in the herb butter and spread evenly over the breast. Lay the bacon over the breast in an overlapping crisscross pattern.

3 Tie the legs together with kitchen string and place the bird on a rack inside a large roasting tin. Roast for 30 minutes, uncovered, then remove from the oven and cover loosely with buttered foil. Reduce the oven temperature to 180ºC, fan 160ºC, gas 4. Continue roasting for 3-3½ hours, basting every 45 minutes with the juices, until cooked through. Remove the foil a few minutes before the end of cooking if the skin still needs to crisp up. To test whether the turkey is cooked, insert a skewer into the thickest part of the leg – the juices should run clear. Transfer to a warmed serving plate, cover loosely with foil and leave to rest for 30 minutes before carving. Leave the oven on.

4 Meanwhile, mix all the stuffing ingredients together in a large bowl and season with salt and freshly ground black pepper. Shape into 20 balls and place in a roasting tin. Place in the oven for 25 minutes, while the turkey is resting.

5 Serve the carved turkey with the stuffing balls and all the trimmings (see overleaf).

Henry VIII is believed to have been the first English king to tuck into turkey

All the trimmings...

A roast turkey dinner wouldn't be complete without all the side dishes. Try this trio of tasty trimmings – roast potatoes, sprouts with pancetta, and maple-glazed carrots and parsnips

Roast potatoes

100g goose fat
2kg King Edward potatoes, peeled and cut into chunks
1 tsp sea salt
4 sprigs of fresh rosemary, leaves only, chopped

1 Preheat the oven to 220°C, fan 200°C, gas 7. Place the goose fat in a large roasting tin and heat in the oven for 10 minutes, until sizzling hot.

2 Meanwhile, place the potatoes in a large pan and cover with cold water. Bring to the boil, then reduce the heat and simmer for 10-12 minutes to parboil. Drain, then return to the pan. Cook, covered, over a low heat for 1-2 minutes, then shake the pan to fluff up the edges. Season with the sea salt.

3 Carefully spoon the potatoes into the hot tin, turning to coat in the goose fat, then sprinkle with the rosemary. Roast for 30-40 minutes, turning occasionally, until crisp and golden.

Serves 10   Prep time: 15 mins   Cook time: 50 mins

Per serving   242 cals, 10.1g fat, 3.3g sat fat, 1.4g total sugars, 0.5g salt

Maple-glazed carrots & parsnips

500g carrots, peeled and quartered lengthways
500g parsnips, peeled and quartered lengthways
50g unsalted butter
100ml white wine
2 tbsp maple syrup

1 Preheat the oven to 200°C, fan 180°C, gas 6. Place the carrots and parsnips in a large roasting tin. Dot with the butter and pour in the wine. Season with salt and freshly ground black pepper and roast for 20 minutes, until just tender.

2 Remove from the oven and drizzle over the maple syrup. Return to the oven and roast for a further 10-15 minutes, until lightly caramelised.

Serves 10   Prep time: 10 mins   Cook time: 35 mins

Per serving   101 cals, 4.8g fat, 2.9g sat fat, 7.9g total sugars, trace salt

Brussels sprouts with pancetta & hazelnuts

1kg Brussels sprouts, trimmed
50g unsalted butter
2 tbsp olive oil
200g shallots, peeled and sliced
2 x 206g pack Sainsbury's Simply Italian cubetti di pancetta
2 sprig of fresh thyme, leaves only
100g blanched hazelnuts, roughly chopped

1 Boil the sprouts for 3-4 minutes, until tender but firm. Drain and run under cold water, then place on a clean tea towel to absorb the excess water.

2 Melt the butter and olive oil in a large, heavy-based frying pan. Add the shallots and gently cook for 5 minutes, then add the pancetta and thyme.

3 Cook for a further 10 minutes, until beginning to crisp. Add the hazelnuts and sprouts to the pan, fry over a high heat for 2-3 minutes to heat through, then serve.

Serves 10
Prep time: 15 mins   Cook time: 25 mins

Per serving   322 cals, 26.6g fat, 8.5g sat fat, 4.2g total sugars, 1.6g salt

Christmas pudding

Steeped in flavour as well as time-honoured tradition, this dreamy Christmas pudding will be the perfect conclusion to your festive feasting

100g each raisins, currants and sultanas
75g ready-to-eat dried figs, chopped
50g chopped mixed peel
1 tsp ground cinnamon
1 tsp mixed spice
½ tsp freshly ground nutmeg
200ml stout
2 tbsp Amaretto liqueur
Zest and juice of 1 orange
25g unsalted butter, plus extra for greasing
250g dark brown soft sugar
25g flaked almonds
50g pecan nuts
25g glacé cherries, chopped
100g light shredded vegetable suet
2 medium eggs, beaten
50g plain flour
100g breadcrumbs

Serves 8
Prep time: 25 mins, plus overnight soaking
Cook time: 6–8 hours

Per serving
538 cals, 19.1g fat, 7.4g sat fat, 69.7g total sugars, 0.3g salt

1 Place the raisins, currants, sultanas, figs and 25g chopped mixed peel in a large bowl with the cinnamon, mixed spice, nutmeg, stout, Amaretto and orange zest and juice. Mix well, then cover and leave overnight in a cool place for the flavours to mature.

2 Heat the butter with 25g sugar in a pan until melted. Stir in the remaining 25g peel, the almonds, pecans and cherries, and arrange in the bottom of a greased 1.2-litre pudding basin.

3 Stir the suet, eggs, flour, breadcrumbs and remaining 225g sugar into the bowl of soaked dried fruit and mix well. Tip into the pudding basin and pack down tightly.

4 Prepare a large steamer or, alternatively, place a trivet or inverted heatproof plate in a large lidded pan. Cut 2 x 70cm lengths of baking parchment and a piece of extra wide foil (turkey foil is ideal). Place the baking parchment lengths on top of the foil, and place the pudding basin in the centre of the parchment. Wrap the pudding, with the foil on the outside. Secure with kitchen string, making a loop for easy removal.

5 Place the pudding in the steamer or pan. Add boiling water, filling to halfway up the sides of the basin. Cover and steam for 6 hours, topping up the water regularly.

6 Remove the pudding from the steamer and discard the foil and parchment. Allow to cool, then rewrap in baking parchment and foil, and store in a cool place for up to 2 months.

7 To reheat, steam for 2 hours, or remove the foil and microwave for 5 minutes.

Stir it up

With origins dating back to the Middle Ages, Christmas pudding has evolved from a kind of spiced porridge made with offcuts of meat and vegetables to a fruit-packed delight. By Victorian times, this 'plum pudding' was a cornerstone of every Christmas dinner – hence the name. The pudding is traditionally made the week before Advent, on 'Stir-up Sunday', when every member of the family works that wooden spoon and makes a wish.

To serve...
To make these even more festive, serve with some brandy cream

Mince pies

As individual as those who make them, these bite-sized beauties encapsulate the season in a pastry case

175g plain flour, plus extra for dusting
100g unsalted butter, chilled and cubed
1 medium egg yolk, beaten
350g mincemeat
Icing sugar, for dusting

Makes 12

**Prep time: 20 mins,
plus chilling time
Cook time: 20 mins**

Per serving
211 cals, 8.9g fat, 5.3g sat fat,
16.9g total sugars, trace salt

(V)

1 In a large bowl, rub the flour into the butter using your fingertips. Make a well in the centre and add the egg yolk and 1 tbsp cold water. Using a knife, work into a dough, adding a drop more water if necessary. Knead gently until smooth. Wrap in clingfilm and chill in the fridge for 15 minutes.

2 Preheat the oven to 200°C, fan 180°C, gas 6.

3 On a floured surface, roll out the pastry to a thickness of 5mm. Using a 7cm round cutter, stamp out 12 rounds. Line a 12-hole tart tin with the pastry rounds and spoon a generous teaspoon of mincemeat into each case. Roll out the pastry trimmings, cut out small stars and trees, and place on top of the mince pies.

4 Bake in the oven for 10 minutes. Reduce the oven temperature to 180°C, fan 160°C, gas 4 and bake for a further 8-10 minutes, until golden. Cool on a wire rack, then dust with icing sugar.

Keep your eyes on the pies

A personal favourite of Father Christmas, the mince pie is the ideal sweet treat to enjoy with a cuppa. However, the first mince pies were savoury creations filled with chopped meat or liver cooked with dried fruit and spices. By the 16th century, 'minced' or 'shred' pies were a Christmas speciality, until Oliver Cromwell put paid to this in 1644 by banning them - he saw them as a symbol of the gluttony that surrounded the festive period. Happily for Santa, those days are long gone. Suet has replaced meat on the ingredients list, but the dried fruit and spices remain.

Afternoon tea

Forget the hectic whirl of daily life and revive the civilising, scone-focused ritual that's a watchword for relaxation. In factories and offices, at home or at large, accept no excuses: no matter what you're doing, everything stops for tea

Cuppas & cream cakes

Whether enjoyed with champagne at the Ritz or a brew in the garden on a summer's afternoon, one thing's for sure: we'll never give up our passion for the great British teatime

A brief history of the British afternoon tea

It's hard to imagine life without afternoon tea, but believe it or not, the practice of bringing together cuppas and cream cakes has only been with us for around 150 years. The brains behind this fabulous match was the Duchess of Bedford, who found herself rather peckish in the hours between luncheon and dinner. She ordered tea, cakes and sandwiches to be brought to her room in the middle of the afternoon and, unsurprisingly, the idea caught on. Before long, genteel ladies in tea gowns and gloves were gathering in drawing rooms across Britain to sample something similar. Today the gloves are off, but dress codes do apply if you happen to be at one of London's finest hotels, such as the Ritz, where afternoon tea is taken to the accompaniment of a grand piano. Keep things casual at home with our recipes for an impressive array of sandwiches, cakes, tarts and macaroons that will have guests flocking around your cake stand. More tea, Vicar?

How to make the perfect cup of tea

- Always use good-quality tea and store it in an airtight container.
- Use freshly drawn water and boil it only once so it contains the maximum amount of oxygen.
- Warm the pot and add one rounded teaspoon (or one tea bag) for each cup you're making.
- Brewing times depend on personal taste and the variety of tea you're using. The UK Tea Council recommends 2-3 minutes for Darjeeling, for example, but 3-4 minutes for Assam.
- The debate continues as to whether or not to put the milk in first, but the general consensus concurs with the Royal Society of Chemistry, which is in favour of starting with the tea. That's how the Queen takes hers, apparently...

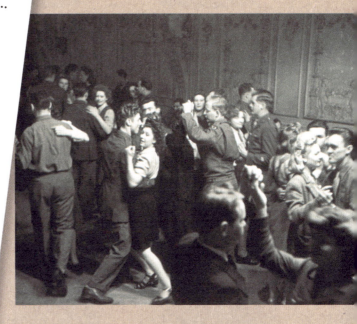

Taking to the dance floor

These days, tea dances are considered rather sedate affairs, for those of retirement age. But it wasn't always so – indeed, there were racy elements, such as meeting and dancing in close proximity to the opposite sex (remember, it was the days before school discos...). Everything was above board, though, as even the Royal Navy would put on tea dances for its young men on board the ship or at a venue ashore, such as a hotel. Local girls would be invited along as dancing partners.

The tea dance appears to have evolved from afternoon tea some time in the late 19th century. It took place around 4pm to 7pm, and refreshment also involved tea, sandwiches, cakes and so on – perhaps with a glass of champagne-cup. Young couples would dance to an orchestra, chaperoned by their elders, who no doubt enjoyed the tea and chat.

By 1910, hotels such as the Waldorf and the Savoy were hosting tea dances, which were previously held at private houses. The same year, the tango debuted in London and its popularity spread like wildfire. The Waldorf caught on, giving lessons and Tango Teas in its magnificent Palm Court.

As the years passed, dance trends changed from the waltz to tango, to the charleston and the Lindy Hop, with some of the music and dance steps brought over by the American soldiers. Tea dances may have declined in popularity since World War II, but young hipsters have donned their dancing shoes and somewhat revived the practice in recent years.

Love at first bite

It was in 1765 that John Montagu, the Fourth Earl of Sandwich (right), first ate the savoury snack to which he gave his name. A hardened gambler, he ordered the cook at his club to bring to the gambling table his favourite salt beef - but tucked between toasted bread slices. He was delighted with the invention, which meant he could eat without getting meat fat on his cards. His snack apparently sparked the cry: 'I'll have the same as Sandwich!'

Finger sandwiches

**These delicate little savouries are a light and delicious opener
to afternoon tea, whetting the appetite for the sweet treats to follow**

Cucumber & mint

2 tbsp finely chopped fresh chives
½ x 28g pack Sainsbury's fresh
mint, leaves picked and finely
chopped
30g unsalted butter, softened
8 slices from a medium-cut
white loaf
½ cucumber, thinly sliced

1 Beat the chives and mint into the butter and leave to chill in the fridge
if too soft.

2 Lightly spread the herb butter on one side of each slice of bread. Pat dry
the cucumber, neatly layer on top and season with a little salt and freshly
ground black pepper. Slice off the crusts and cut each sandwich into quarters.

Makes 4 sandwiches or 16 quarters Prep time: 15 mins

Per sandwich 210 cals, 7.6g fat, 4.2g sat fat, 3.1g total sugars, 0.5g salt

Egg mayonnaise

4 medium eggs
15g unsalted butter, softened
8 slices from a medium-cut
seeded granary loaf
100g light mayonnaise
2 tbsp salad cream
1 tbsp wholegrain mustard
40g watercress, leaves picked

1 Place the eggs in a large pan of boiling water and boil for 6–8 minutes.
When cooked, plunge into cold water and allow to cool.

2 Meanwhile, lightly butter the bread. Peel and chop the eggs, and place in
a medium bowl with the mayonnaise, salad cream and mustard. Season
with salt and freshly ground black pepper, and mix well. Spread the egg
mayonnaise on 4 slices of bread, then top each with watercress and another
slice of bread. Slice off the crusts and cut each sandwich into 3 fingers.

Makes 4 sandwiches or 12 fingers Prep time: 15 mins

Per sandwich 374 cals, 24.3g fat, 5.2g sat fat, 5.9g total sugars, 1.9g salt

Smoked salmon & cream cheese

150g light soft cheese
2 tbsp capers, rinsed, drained and chopped
2 tbsp chopped fresh dill
Zest of 1 lemon and 1 tbsp juice
30g unsalted butter, softened
8 slices from a Taste the Difference soft
wholemeal farmhouse batch loaf
200g thinly sliced smoked salmon

1 In a small bowl, mix together the soft
cheese, capers, dill, lemon zest, lemon juice
and lots of freshly ground black pepper.
2 Lightly butter 4 slices of bread and lay
the salmon over, filling right to the edges.
Spread the cheese mixture over the
4 unbuttered slices of bread, and sandwich
together with the salmon. Slice off the
crusts and cut each sandwich into 3 fingers.

Makes 4 sandwiches or 12 fingers
Prep time: 15 mins

Per sandwich 371 cals, 21.8g fat,
8.7g sat fat, 3.8g total sugars, 3.4g salt

This champion of cakes has graced a thousand afternoon teas and village fêtes

Victoria sandwich

Invented to cheer up a queen and still the star of the tea party, this feather-light cake is an all-round crowd-pleaser

½ tsp vegetable oil, for greasing
170g unsalted butter, softened
170g caster sugar
4 medium eggs, lightly beaten
170g plain flour, sifted
2 tsp baking powder, sifted
3 tbsp raspberry jam
1 tsp icing sugar, for dusting

Serves 8
Prep time: 15 mins,
plus cooling time
Cook time: 25 mins

Per serving
385 cals, 21g fat,
12.4g sat fat, 27.1g total
sugars, 0.6g salt

(V)

1 Preheat the oven to 180ºC, fan 160ºC, gas 4. Grease 2 x 18cm round cake tins with oil, then line the base of each with baking parchment.

2 Cream together the butter and sugar until light and fluffy. Gradually add the egg, a little at a time, beating well after each addition. Fold in the flour and baking powder, and stir in 3 tbsp water to bring the mixture to a dropping consistency.

3 Divide the mixture between the 2 tins and bake on the middle shelf of the oven for 25 minutes, until well risen and golden.

4 Leave the cakes to cool slightly in their tins, then remove the base liners and transfer to a wire rack to cool completely.

5 Sandwich the cakes together with the jam and sift the icing sugar over the top.

Cook's note: if you're feeling decadent, spread 6 tbsp whipped cream over the jam before sandwiching the cakes together

Sponge or sandwich?

There's some debate over the correct name for this British teatime classic, with some experts pointing out that a true sponge contains no fat. What's sure is that the Victoria sandwich, doyenne of the village fête, was named in honour of Queen Victoria. In mourning after the death of her husband, Prince Albert, in 1861, the Queen (pictured above with Albert) retreated to her Isle of Wight home, where she was encouraged to give tea parties, and the Victoria sandwich was born. It was a new invention, baking powder, that gave the cake its heavenly rise.

Melting moments

These will-o'-the-wisp biscuits, flavoured with vanilla, orange or chocolate, are so tempting they'll disappear in minutes

170g slightly salted butter, softened
60g icing sugar
170g plain flour, plus extra for dusting
60g cornflour
1 tsp vanilla extract

For the filling
80g slightly salted butter, softened
80g icing sugar, sifted
Juice of 1 ripe passion fruit (strained of seeds, if you like)

Makes 8
Prep time: 15 mins, plus cooling time
Cook time: 15 mins

....

Each biscuit
410 cals, 26g fat, 16g sat fat, 18.9g total sugars, 0.6g salt

1 Preheat the oven to 180°C, fan 160°C, gas 4.

2 In a large bowl, beat together the butter and icing sugar until light and fluffy. Add the flour, cornflour and vanilla extract, and beat again until the mixture just comes together.

3 Using your hands, roll the mixture into 16 balls, then flatten into discs. Place on 2 baking trays lined with baking parchment. Using a lightly floured fork, press down gently on the top of each biscuit to create a pattern. Bake for 12-14 minutes, until just starting to turn golden, then cool on a wire rack.

4 To make the filling, beat together the butter, icing sugar and juice until creamy. Use to sandwich together the biscuit halves.

Cook's note: to make orange melting moments, substitute the passion fruit for the zest of 1 orange and 1 tbsp freshly squeezed orange juice. For a chocolate variation, substitute the passion fruit for 1 tbsp cocoa powder mixed with 1 tbsp water

Carrot cake

**For a sweet treat with an unusual ingredient and an interesting past,
this sublime sponge with cream-cheese icing is a sure-fire winner**

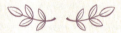

For the cake
Butter, for greasing
300ml sunflower oil
100g soft dark brown sugar
250g light muscovado sugar
3 large eggs
175g plain flour, sifted
¾ tsp baking powder
¾ tsp bicarbonate of soda
¾ tsp ground cinnamon
Pinch of salt
225g carrot, grated
75g walnuts, chopped
50g sultanas (optional)

For the icing
250g light cream cheese,
at room temperature
150g unsalted butter, softened
Seeds of 1 vanilla pod
75g icing sugar, sifted
¼ tsp cinnamon

Serves 12
Prep time: 25 mins, plus cooling
and chilling time
Cook time: 1¼ hours

Per serving
636 cals, 44.3g fat, 12.4g sat fat,
19.8g total sugars, 0.8g salt

1 Preheat the oven to 180°C, fan 160°C, gas 4. Butter a deep 23cm spring-form tin and line with baking parchment.

2 Pour the oil into a large bowl, add both the sugars and beat with an electric hand whisk until well mixed. Add the eggs one at a time, beating well after each addition.

3 Fold in the flour, baking powder, bicarbonate of soda, cinnamon and salt, then carefully fold in the carrot, walnuts and sultanas (if using). Tip into the prepared tin and smooth the surface.

4 Place in the preheated oven and bake on the middle shelf for 45 minutes. Reduce the oven temperature to 160°C, fan 140°C, gas 3 and bake for a further 30 minutes, until a skewer comes out clean when inserted into the middle of the cake. Leave to cool in the tin for 10 minutes before turning out onto a wire rack to cool completely.

5 For the icing, using a whisk or a food processor, blend the cream cheese, butter and vanilla seeds until smooth, then add the icing sugar and blend again. Chill in the fridge for 30 minutes.

6 Using a palette knife, ice the top and sides of the cake, then sprinkle with the cinnamon.

What's up, Doc?

Carrot cake originated in medieval times in Sweden, when canny cooks discovered that the humble carrot, sweeter than any other vegetable besides the sugar beet, could be used in place of more conventional sweeteners, which were scarce and expensive. Its popularity was revived in Britain during World War II, when sugar was rationed, and it's still a hit today, being voted the country's favourite cake in a recent nationwide poll.

253

Strawberry tarts

Deliciously delightful, these fruit-filled fancies might have come fresh from the oven of the Queen of Hearts

175g plain flour, plus extra for dusting
100g unsalted butter, chilled and cubed
70g caster sugar
1 medium egg yolk
100ml double cream
200g mascarpone
Seeds of 1 vanilla pod
1 x 400g pack Sainsbury's strawberries, hulled and sliced
2 tbsp apricot jam, melted

Serves 8
Prep time: 20 mins, plus chilling time
Cook time: 15 mins

Each tart
405 cals, 27.7g fat, 17.9g sat fat, 17g total sugars, trace salt

1 To make the pastry, sift the flour into a bowl. Lightly rub in the butter with your fingertips, until the mixture resembles breadcrumbs. Stir in 30g sugar. Make a well in the mixture and add the egg yolk and 1 tbsp cold water. Use a round-bladed knife to bring everything together, adding a drop more water if necessary. Use your hands to form a dough, handling it as little as possible. (Alternatively, make the pastry in a food processor.) Wrap in clingfilm and chill in the fridge for 20 minutes.

2 Roll out the pastry on a lightly floured surface. Using a 6-7cm fluted cutter, cut out 8 rounds and use to line a cupcake tin. Chill in the fridge for 20 minutes. Meanwhile, preheat the oven to 190°C, fan 170°C, gas 5.

3 Line the pastry with circles of baking parchment, then fill with baking beans or uncooked rice and bake blind for 10 minutes. Remove the beans or rice and the baking parchment, and bake for a further 2-3 minutes, until crisp and golden. Leave to cool.

4 Whisk together the cream, mascarpone, vanilla seeds and remaining 40g sugar. Spoon the mascarpone mixture into the pastry cases and top with the strawberries. Brush with the melted apricot jam. Serve on the day of making.

Top tip...
Short of time? Use 375g Sainsbury's ready rolled shortcrust pastry

Off with their heads!

When the Knave of Hearts stole the Queen's tarts in the 18th-century nursery rhyme – a story Lewis Carroll reprised 100 years later in *Alice in Wonderland* – he must have been very hungry indeed, because his punishment would have been most severe. Not only, as the ditty tells us, was he beaten 'full sore' by the King, but the crime of theft from royalty would have been treated as treason and cost him his life. Let's hope the tarts were worth it!

Coffee & walnut cake

With layers of airy sponge and sweet buttercream balanced by decadent coffee and walnut flavours, this cake is simply divine

2 tbsp instant coffee granules
200g unsalted butter, softened plus extra for greasing
200g golden caster sugar
4 medium eggs
200g self-raising flour
1 tsp baking powder
1 x 100g pack Sainsbury's walnut halves, roughly chopped

For the icing
2 tsp instant coffee granules
150g unsalted butter, softened
300g icing sugar, sifted

Serves 12
Prep time: 15 mins, plus cooling time
Cook time: 25 mins

Per serving
535 cals, 32.3g fat, 17.1g sat fat, 42.9g total sugars, 0.3g salt

V

1 Preheat the oven to 180°C, fan 160°C, gas 4. Grease 2 x 20cm round cake tins and line with baking parchment. Dissolve the coffee granules in 1 tbsp boiling water and allow to cool.

2 Beat together the butter and sugar until light and fluffy, then add the eggs, one at a time, beating well after each addition. Using a large spoon, fold in the flour and baking powder. Stir in 75g walnuts and the coffee mixture.

3 Divide the mixture between the 2 cake tins and bake on the middle shelf of the oven for 20-25 minutes, until golden and springy to the touch. Remove the cakes from the tins and leave on a wire rack to cool completely.

4 To make the icing, dissolve the coffee granules in 1 tbsp boiling water. Beat together the butter and icing sugar until pale and fluffy, then add the coffee mixture and beat until well combined. Use half the icing to sandwich the cakes together. Cover the top with the remaining icing and decorate with the remaining 25g walnuts.

What better partner for a pick-me-up cup of coffee?

Macaroons

Cupcakes and whoopie pies had their moment, but macaroons have no match when it comes to classic, unashamedly girlie chic

150g icing sugar
100g ground almonds
A few drops of yellow, red and green food colouring
2 large egg whites (about 75g)
Pinch of cream of tartar
60g caster sugar
½ tsp vanilla extract

For the filling

150g unsalted butter, softened
125g icing sugar
A few drops of yellow, red and green food colouring
A few drops of flavour extracts such as lemon, rose or peppermint (optional)

Makes 20

**Prep time: 20 mins, plus standing time
Cook time: 20 mins**

....

Per macaroon

159 cals, 8.9g fat, 4.3g sat fat, 17.7g total sugars, trace salt

1 Line 2 baking trays with non-stick silicone paper or baking parchment. In a food processor, whizz the icing sugar and almonds to a fine powder. Sift evenly into 3 separate bowls and add different colouring to each.

2 In a separate bowl, whisk the egg whites with the cream of tartar until medium peaks form. Slowly add the caster sugar, a spoonful at a time. Add the vanilla extract and whisk until thick and glossy.

3 Slowly fold one-third of the meringue into each of the bowls containing the almond mixture until completely combined. Keep folding until the mixture deflates quite a bit and creates a ribbon effect for about 20 seconds when it falls from the spoon.

4 Preheat the oven to 150ºC, fan 130ºC, gas 2.

5 Spoon into 3 separate piping bags, each with a 1cm plain nozzle. Pipe small equal rounds – about 3cm each, spaced 2cm apart – onto the baking trays. Tap the baking trays hard several times to remove any bubbles and to flatten the macaroons into the shape shown in the photo (opposite). Allow to stand for 20 minutes to form a slight skin.

6 Cook the macaroons in the middle of the oven for 20 minutes.

7 In the meantime, make the fillings. In a medium-sized bowl, beat the butter until light and fluffy, then beat in the icing sugar. Spoon the mixture into 3 small bowls and stir a different colouring and your chosen flavour extracts, if desired, into each. Use the buttercream to sandwich together pairs of macaroons and serve at once.

Street parties

There's no better way to celebrate national events than with a good old-fashioned knees-up and, across the country, we've been letting our hair down at street parties for generations. Just add music, food and a little liquid refreshment for an afternoon to remember

Roll out the barrel

There's lots to celebrate in 2012, so get together with your neighbours, cook up some of our great recipes and let's all have a party

Dust down the trestle tables, untangle the bunting and dig out that Chas & Dave CD – it's time to celebrate! Nobody does street parties like the British. We all remember (or have at least heard about) the big bashes held for the Queen's silver jubilee in 1977 and Charles and Diana's royal wedding in 1981. Not to mention the fabulous dos, still fresh in the mind, that marked the marriage of William and Kate. But you may not realise that street parties date back to 1919, when 'peace teas' were held to mark the signing of the Versailles peace treaty after World War I. They were a special treat for children in a time of great hardship.

Since then, there have been plenty of reasons to hang out the Union Jack flags: the coronations (of George VI in 1937 and our present Queen in 1953), VE day in 1945, the Festival of Britain in 1951 and England's World Cup victory in 1966 were all events that had the nation buttering up the sarnies, donning silly hats and getting into the party spirit. And 2012 is bound to be a bumper year for community get-togethers up and down the land, thanks to the Queen's diamond jubilee and the much-anticipated London 2012 Olympic and Paralympic games. What better excuses for a party?

1953 The Queen's coronation

**1981
The wedding of
Charles and Diana**

**1977
The Queen's
silver jubilee**

**1966
England won
the World Cup**

How to take the stress out of a street party

1 Invite all the neighbours, even (or especially) those you don't know.

2 Let the council know your plans in plenty of time, three to 12 weeks before the big day. You often don't need a permit, but it's sensible to keep everyone informed. For practical information, visit the Streets Alive website at streetparty.org.uk.

3 Work out what you'll do if it rains. Can you retreat to a church or community hall? If not, buy or borrow a few gazebos to protect the food and remind everyone to bring a brolly.

4 Plan some simple games to keep the kids entertained – think along the lines of a sports day with sack races, egg-and-spoon, etc. You could even stage your own mini-Olympics!

5 Get everyone to agree on what they're making beforehand so you get a good variety of food. And ask for volunteers to help with the clean-up, too.

Top tip... Serve with slices of crusty bread and let everyone help themselves

Fit for a Queen

Coronation chicken was first served at the banquet held after Elizabeth was crowned in 1953. Curry powder, a fairly exotic ingredient in the 1950s, was included as a nod to the Queen's role as colonial ruler. The recipe was easy to prepare and inexpensive – just the ticket in ration-bound Britain. Who'd have guessed it would still be topping jacket potatoes across the land 60 years on.

Coronation chicken

They'll be dancing in the street for these – a tasty chicken recipe originally created for the Queen's coronation, and our updated version to celebrate the diamond jubilee

1.7kg chicken, skin removed
1 tbsp vegetable oil
½ onion, finely chopped
1 tbsp medium curry powder, plus a pinch to garnish
1 tsp tomato purée
150ml red wine
1 dried bay leaf
Juice of ½ lemon
50g dried, ready-to-eat apricots, chopped
300ml mayonnaise
3 tbsp single cream, lightly whipped
1 x 75g bag Sainsbury's watercress
25g toasted flaked almonds

Serves 6
Prep time: 15 mins
Cook time: 1¼ hours

Per serving
615 cals, 48.9g fat, 6.4g sat fat, 5.5g total sugars, 0.9g salt

1 Place the chicken in a large saucepan and cover with water. Simmer over a low heat for 1¼ hours, until cooked. Carefully remove the chicken and leave to cool.

2 Meanwhile, heat the oil in a large saucepan, then add the onion and soften for 3–4 minutes. Stir through the curry powder and cook for a further 1–2 minutes. Add the tomato purée, wine, bay leaf, lemon juice, apricots and 100ml cold water. Bring to the boil, then gently simmer, uncovered, for 5 minutes until thickened. Place in a food processor, add 3 tbsp cold water and blend until smooth. Leave to cool.

3 Tear the chicken from the bones and place in a large bowl. In another bowl, mix together the curry purée, mayonnaise and whipped cream. Fold through the chicken until well coated.

4 Serve the chicken on a bed of watercress, garnished with flaked almonds and a sprinkle of curry powder.

Jubilee chicken

Poach a 1.7kg chicken, skin removed, as in the recipe for coronation chicken (left), and set aside to cool. In the meantime, in a large bowl, mix together 300ml half-fat crème fraîche, 1 tbsp lemon juice, the zest of ½ lemon, 1 finely chopped shallot, 1 tbsp red wine vinegar, 1 tsp honey, ½ tsp ground coriander and 1 tbsp wholegrain mustard. Tear the chicken from the bones, then dice and stir through the crème fraîche mixture. Serve on a bed of little gem lettuce leaves and sprinkle with rocket leaves.

Serves 6
Prep time: 10 mins   Cook time: 1¼ hours

Per serving 308 cals, 16.5g fat, 7.4g sat fat, 2.6g total sugars, 0.3g salt

Asparagus tarts

These individual savoury tarts look really impressive and are super-easy to make

700g asparagus spears, woody part broken off
100g basics Italian hard cheese
150g crème fraîche
1 x 500g block Sainsbury's puff pastry
2 tbsp olive oil
1 medium egg, beaten

Makes 8
Prep time: 10 mins
Cook time: 20 mins

Per tart
391 cals, 28.4g fat, 15.6g sat fat, 2.9g total sugars, 0.5g salt

1 Preheat the oven to 200°C, fan 180°C, gas 6. Cook the asparagus in a pan of simmering water for 1 minute, then drain and plunge into cold water. Drain again and set aside.

2 Using a vegetable peeler, shave 25g Italian hard cheese and set aside. Finely grate the remaining 75g cheese and mix into the crème fraîche.

3 Roll out the pastry to a 32cm square. Cut into 8 rectangles, each measuring 16 x 8cm, and place on 2 baking trays. Using a sharp knife, score a border on each tart, 1cm from the edge, being careful not to cut all the way through. Spread the crème fraîche mixture inside each border.

4 Divide the asparagus between the 8 tarts and drizzle with olive oil. Brush the edges of the tarts with the beaten egg and bake for 20 minutes, until golden. Scatter over the reserved cheese shavings, season to taste with freshly ground black pepper and serve.

Top tip...
For one big tart, use a whole sheet of Sainsbury's ready rolled puff pastry

Top tip...
This is also great
for picnics – wrap
in foil and pack
in a cool-bag

Jumbo sausage roll

Sausage rolls are classic street-party fare, so go large with this herby, loaf-sized version – it will make a fantastic centrepiece

700g Taste the Difference Lincolnshire pork sausages
1 onion, finely chopped
150g dried ready-to-eat apricots, finely chopped
1 x 28g pack Sainsbury's fresh flat-leaf parsley, chopped
2 sprigs fresh sage, chopped
100g fresh white breadcrumbs
1 x 500g block Sainsbury's puff pastry
1 medium egg, beaten

Serves 12
Prep time: 20 mins, plus resting time
Cook time: 45 mins

Per slice
428 cals, 28.7g fat, 10.7g sat fat, 6.8g total sugars, 0.6g salt

1 Preheat the oven to 180ºC, fan 160ºC, gas 4. Squeeze the sausagemeat from the sausages into a bowl. Stir in the onion, apricots, parsley, sage and breadcrumbs. Season with salt and freshly ground black pepper and mix until fully combined.

2 Roll out the pastry to a 26 x 40cm rectangle, 3mm thick, and trim if necessary. Shape the sausage mixture into a fat roll and place lengthways across the centre of the pastry, leaving 2.5cm free at each end. Brush the edges of the pastry with some of the beaten egg. Fold over the top and bottom halves to cover the filling and form a roll, and secure. Gently pinch the ends together to seal, and trim if necessary.

3 Place on a baking tray, with the pastry seam on the bottom. Brush with the remaining egg. Using a sharp knife, cut slashes in the pastry at 3cm intervals. Bake for 45 minutes, until deep golden. Remove and leave to rest for 10 minutes before slicing and serving, or allow to cool completely and serve in slices.

Cheese & chilli nachos

Preheat the oven to 200ºC, fan 180ºC, gas 6. Tip ½ x 200g pack tortilla chips into an ovenproof dish and layer with ½ x 230g pot salsa, ½ x 335g pack cherry tomatoes, halved, 2 sliced spring onions, 100g grated Cheddar and a sprinkling of crushed chillies. Repeat this process and bake for 15 minutes, until the cheese begins to melt. Remove and sprinkle with another chopped spring onion. Great served warm with extra salsa, soured cream and guacamole.

Serves 8
Prep time: 10 mins Cook time: 15 mins

Per serving 256 cals, 15.8g fat, 6.1g sat fat, 4.9g total sugars, 1.3g salt

Top tip...

Bake these, then wrap in foil to keep them warm until party time

Pork & apricot parcels

A combination of sweet and savoury, these yummy parcels are seasoned with fragrant herbs and sprinkled with crunchy seeds

1 tsp olive oil
½ onion, chopped
½ carrot, peeled and grated
½ x 500g pack Sainsbury's be good to yourself extra lean British pork mince
5 dried, ready-to-eat apricots, finely chopped
1 tsp fresh rosemary, leaves chopped
8 sheets fresh, ready-rolled filo pastry
50g slightly salted butter, melted
1 tsp sesame seeds
1 tsp poppy seeds

Makes 8
Prep time: 20 mins
Cook time: 30 mins

Per parcel
222 cals, 8.9g fat, 4.1g sat fat, 2.9g total sugars, 0.2g salt

1 Heat the oil in a small pan. Fry the onion, stirring, for 5 minutes, until it softens and starts to turn golden.

2 Stir in the carrot and cook for another minute. Transfer to a bowl, then stir in the mince, apricots and rosemary. Using your hands, mix well, then divide into 8 portions.

3 Preheat the oven to 180°C, fan 160°C, gas 4. Lay out 1 sheet of filo and brush half of it lengthways with a little butter. Fold the pastry in half lengthways to make one long strip. Place 1 portion of the pork mixture at one end. Fold the pastry and filling over at right angles to make a triangle, and continue folding to form a neat triangular parcel. Seal with a little melted butter. Repeat with the remaining pastry and pork mixture to make 8 parcels.

4 Place on a baking tray, brush with the remaining butter and sprinkle with the sesame and poppy seeds. Bake for 20-25 minutes, until the parcels are crisp and golden.

Courgette frittata

Boil 500g baby new potatoes with a mint sprig for 10-15 minutes, until tender. Drain, cool and thickly slice. Melt 25g unsalted butter in a frying pan. Add 2 grated courgettes and cook, stirring, for 3 minutes, then add 150g frozen peas and cook for a further 2 minutes. Remove from the heat and stir in the potatoes and 1 tbsp chopped fresh mint. Tip into a roasting tin lined with baking parchment. Preheat the oven to 180°C, fan 160°C, gas 4. Beat 6 large eggs with 75g grated mature Cheddar. Season with salt and freshly ground black pepper, pour into the tin and sprinkle over 1 tbsp grated basics hard Italian cheese. Bake for 20-25 minutes, until set. Cool, then cut into squares.

Serves 8
Prep time: 15 mins
Cook time: 45 mins

Per serving 203 cals, 12.2g fat, 5.6g sat fat, 1.6g total sugars, 0.4g salt

Gourmet hot dogs

Barbecues are ideal for feeding the hungry hordes at a street party, and these meaty morsels can be cooked on the barbie or indoors

1 ½ tbsp honey
2 tsp ground cumin
8 Taste the Difference ultimate outdoor-bred pork sausages
8 Sainsbury's large multi-seeded deli sandwich rolls, split in half
1 x 100g bag Sainsbury's Italian-style salad

For the houmous
1 x 410g tin Sainsbury's chick peas, drained
2 tbsp lemon juice
2 cloves garlic, crushed
1 tsp ground cumin
100g tahini paste
2 tbsp olive oil
Pinch of paprika

Serves 8
Prep time: 15 mins
Cook time: 15 mins
....
Per serving
539 cals, 29.7g fat,
7.8g sat fat, 7g total sugars,
1.5g salt

1 Preheat the barbecue or grill to high.

2 Place all the ingredients for the houmous in a food processor along with 4 tbsp water. Whizz until smooth.

3 Mix the honey and cumin together, then brush it on the sausages. Barbecue or grill, turning every 5 minutes, for about 15 minutes, until golden.

4 Spread 2 tbsp houmous onto each roll (store any leftover houmous in the fridge) and add a small handful of salad leaves. Pop in the sausages and serve.

Sweet soy drumsticks

In a bowl, mix together 75ml light soy sauce, 1 tbsp vegetable oil, 3 tbsp runny honey and 1 crushed clove garlic. Place 8 Sainsbury's chicken drumsticks in a large bowl, pour over the marinade and leave in the fridge for 1 hour, or overnight if you have time, turning once. Cook the drumsticks for 30-35 minutes on a barbecue preheated to high or in a roasting tin in an oven preheated to 200°C, fan 180°C, gas 6.

Serves 8
Prep time: 5 mins, plus marinating time
Cook time: 35 mins
....
Per drumstick
133 cals, 3.7g fat, 0.8g sat fat,
7.8g total sugars, 2.9g salt

A flaming good idea

In the 1600s, a barbecue was where you'd lay your head at the end of the day, not sizzle your sausages. A wooden framework for sleeping on, it evolved into a contraption on which to dry fish in order to preserve them. In a triumph of optimism over experience, barbecues as we know them today first became popular during the 1960s - despite the British weather.

Lamb patties
(with mint yogurt sauce)

Give partygoers the thrill of the grill with these tasty barbecue recipes, including a fab veggie option, or cook them indoors if you prefer

1 x 500g pack Sainsbury's lamb mince
2 tbsp mint jelly
2 tsp cumin seeds, crushed
1 medium egg, beaten
50g fresh breadcrumbs
100ml Sainsbury's be good to yourself Greek style natural yogurt
2 tbsp chopped fresh mint
1 tbsp olive oil
4 pitta breads, split and halved
1 x 80g bag Sainsbury's cosmopolitan salad
120g cherry tomatoes, halved

Makes 8
Prep time: 15 mins, plus chilling time
Cook time: 20 mins

Per serving
315 cals, 15.4g fat, 6.9g sat fat, 5.9g total sugars, 0.4g salt

1 Preheat the barbecue or grill to medium-high.

2 Combine the mince, mint jelly, cumin seeds, egg and breadcrumbs in a large bowl. Season with salt and freshly ground black pepper and shape into 8 small patties. Chill in the fridge for 10 minutes.

3 Meanwhile, pour the yogurt into a small bowl and mix in the mint. Season with salt and freshly ground black pepper and set aside.

4 Brush the patties with the olive oil, then cook over the grill or barbecue for 15-20 minutes, turning once, until cooked through. Meanwhile, toast the pitta breads.

5 Serve the patties in the toasted pittas with the minty yogurt sauce, salad and tomatoes.

Halloumi kebabs

Spear 250g halloumi, cubed, onto 8 metal skewers with 1 deseeded and chopped red pepper, 16 small peeled shallots and 16 small mushrooms. Place on a large plate. In a small bowl, whisk together 4 tbsp lemon juice, 120ml olive oil, 1 x 28g pack fresh mint, chopped, and a few crushed chillies. Drizzle over the skewers, turn and marinate for 10 minutes. Heat the barbecue or grill to medium-high and cook the skewers for 10 minutes, turning once, until the vegetables start to soften and char. Drizzle over the remaining marinade and serve.

Serves 8
Prep time: 10 mins, plus marinating time
Cook time: 10 mins

Per serving 258 cals, 23.6g fat, 7.4g sat fat, 3.5g total sugars, 0.9g salt

Serve your trifle in a large glass bowl to show off its tempting layers

Trifle

Fruity, boozy and creamy, this indulgent crowd-pleaser has it all. Leave out the cherry brandy for a child-friendly version

6 medium egg yolks
50g caster sugar
2 tbsp cornflour
900ml double cream
1 vanilla pod, split lengthways
and seeds scraped out
150g each blueberries, blackberries,
small strawberries and raspberries
50g icing sugar
6 tbsp cherry brandy
1 x 365g Sainsbury's strawberry
& vanilla jumbo Swiss roll
80g amaretti biscuits

Serves 10
Prep time: 25 mins, plus infusing, chilling and soaking time
Cook time: 20 mins

....

Per serving
714 cals, 52.4g fat, 29.7g sat fat, 38.1g total sugars, 0.2g salt

1 First, make the custard. In a large bowl, whisk the egg yolks with the sugar until really thick and pale, then stir in the cornflour.

2 Heat 600ml cream in a pan until nearly boiling. Remove from the heat, then add the vanilla seeds and pod, cover and leave to infuse for 15 minutes.

3 Remove the vanilla pod and reheat the cream to boiling point, then strain into the egg mixture, whisking as you pour. Tip into a clean pan and stir with a wooden spoon over a gentle heat for 5-10 minutes, until thickened, then remove from the heat. Transfer to a bowl and cover with clingfilm to prevent a skin forming. Set aside to cool completely, then pop into the fridge to chill, preferably overnight.

4 Place the blueberries, blackberries, strawberries and just over half the raspberries in a large bowl. Sprinkle over the icing sugar and cherry brandy and leave to soak for about 1 hour.

5 Thinly slice the Swiss roll and place in the bottom and around the sides of a 2.5-litre glass serving bowl. Spoon over the fruit and juices. Roughly crush the amaretti biscuits and scatter over the fruit, reserving about 10g to decorate. Spoon the custard over the top in an even layer.

6 Whip the remaining 300ml cream until soft peaks form, then spoon on top of the trifle. Decorate with the reserved raspberries and crushed amaretti biscuits. Chill for at least 1 hour, or overnight if you have time. Remove from the fridge 30 minutes before serving.

'Tis but a trifle

The word trifle comes from the French *trufle*, meaning something whimsical, which seems appropriate for such a charming pudding. Trifles were first mentioned in print in the 16th century, but it wasn't until 1751 that the practice of soaking the sponge or fruit in alcohol got a look-in. This method was used in other desserts, too, such as the amusingly named tipsy cake and hedgehog pudding, which have long since been lost in the mists of time.

Celebration cupcakes

Wave the flag for Britain with these cute treats – their Union Jack decorations are the icing on the cake

60g unsalted butter, softened
125g caster sugar
1 medium egg
130g self-raising flour
60g ground almonds
100ml semi-skimmed milk
100g ready-to-roll blue icing
50g ready-to-roll white icing
50g ready-to-roll red icing
2 tbsp strawberry jam

Makes 12
Prep time: 45 mins
Cook time: 20 mins
....
Per serving
238 cals, 8.7g fat, 3.8g sat fat, 28g total sugars, 0.1g salt

1 Preheat the oven to 180°C, fan 160°C, gas 4. Line a 12-hole cupcake tin with paper cases (we've used Sainsbury's patterned cake cases).

2 Place the butter and sugar in a large bowl and beat until light and fluffy, then whisk in the egg.

3 Mix the flour and ground almonds together in a separate bowl, then mix into the butter mixture. Stir in the milk, then spoon into the paper cases and bake for 20 minutes, until a skewer inserted into the centre of one of the cupcakes comes out clean. Leave to cool on a wire rack.

4 Meanwhile, roll out the blue icing and cut out 12 circles using a 6cm cutter. Roll out the white icing and cut out 48 strips, each measuring 0.75 x 6cm. Roll out the red icing and cut out 48 strips, each measuring 0.5 x 6cm.

5 Once the cakes are cool, brush them with the jam and top each with a blue icing circle. Brush the strips of white icing with a little water and arrange 4 on each cake. Arrange the red strips on top to resemble a British flag.

War-Time
COOKERY
to save fuel and food value

Issued in the National Food Campaign Exhibition
1940

Three cheers...

This trio of beverages – two traditional soft drinks and a cheeky
cocktail – will put some sparkle into your celebrations

Traditional lemonade

4 large unwaxed lemons, plus extra
slices to garnish

100-125g caster sugar, to taste
900ml chilled still or sparkling water

1 Finely grate the zest of the lemons into a saucepan, then squeeze in their
juice. Stir in the sugar, add 100ml water and heat gently until the sugar has
dissolved. Leave to cool.

2 Strain through a fine sieve into a large jug and chill until ready to use.
To serve, add ice, lemon slices and top up with the chilled water. If using
sparkling water, add a good splash first, then stir, to stop it fizzing up too
much, before topping up the jug.

Serves 4
Prep time: 5 mins, plus infusing and chilling time   Cook time: 10 mins

Cheat's ginger beer

Zest and juice of 2 lemons
1 tbsp clear honey
100g fresh ginger, peeled and grated,
plus a few slices to decorate

75g caster sugar
1 litre soda water

1 In a large jug, mix the lemon zest and juice with the honey, ginger and
sugar, then add 100ml soda water. Stir and leave to infuse for 10 minutes.

2 Top up with the remaining 900ml soda water and stir. Slowly pass the
ginger beer through a fine sieve. Serve immediately over ice and decorate
with a fresh slice of ginger, or take a funnel and pour into individual sterilised
bottles and chill until required. Store in the fridge for up to 24 hours.

Serves 4   Prep time: 10 mins, plus infusing time

Jubilee cocktail

1 medium egg white
2 tbsp caster sugar
60ml blackcurrant liqueur (crème de cassis)
Champagne or cava, to top up
Summer berries, to garnish

1 Tip the egg white onto one saucer and
the sugar onto another. Dip the rim of
6 champagne glasses into each in turn.

2 Pour 2 tsp blackcurrant liqueur into each
glass and top up with champagne or cava.

3 Pop a few summer berries into each
glass and serve.

Cook's note: this recipe contains raw eggs

Serves 6   Prep time: 5 mins

The great British picnic

The weather may do its best to put us off, but picnics have been part of the British summer for centuries. Whether it's keeping the sand off our sarnies at the seaside or waving away wasps at the park, nothing beats the laidback fun of sitting on a picnic rug and enjoying food with friends and family

Five fantastic
picnic spots

With beautiful countryside and a stunning coastline on our doorstep, we're spoilt for choice when it comes to places to eat alfresco. Here are a few of the best...

Barafundle Beach, Pembrokeshire

With its soft, golden sands and crystal-clear waters, it's no surprise that this unspoilt beach has been voted one of the best beaches in Britain. The small bay is backed by sand dunes, and there are rock pools and caves to explore when the tide is out - an idyllic location for an outdoor feast.

Did you know?

In 14th-century England, the first picnics would have been hunting feasts, when the food - baked meats and pastries - was shared outdoors before the hunt began. In Victorian times, the picnic craze really took off and the popularity of eating alfresco was reflected in the literature of the era. Mrs Twinkleton contributed 'herself and a veal pie' to a picnic in *The Mystery of Edwin Drood* by Charles Dickens, while in Jane Austen's *Emma*, the matchmaking heroine picnics at Box Hill, in the North Downs - a popular picnic spot to this day.

Yorkshire Sculpture Park, Wakefield

Share your lunch with the sculptures dotted around the lush Bretton Estate. Explore fascinating open-air displays by some of the world's finest artists, set in the natural beauty of a 500-acre historic estate. Admission is free (you just pay for the parking) and picnicking is permitted in specific areas.

St Herbert's Island, Cumbria

Inject a sense of adventure into your picnic – hire a rowing boat at Keswick launch and head across to the uninhabited St Herbert's Island in the middle of Derwentwater. There are five acres of woodland to explore, then you can picnic on the pebbly beach before working off lunch as you row back to the mainland.

Somehow food always tastes better enjoyed outdoors

Loch an Eilein, Rothiemurchus

In the heart of the Cairngorms National Park, near Aviemore, in the Scottish Highlands, this beautiful place has been voted Britain's best picnic spot, and it's easy to see why. You can take a walk around the loch and enjoy the breathtaking

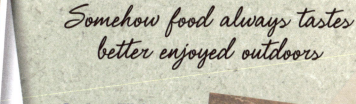

scenery, with dramatic views of the mountains and the ruined castle on the island. If you're lucky, you may also see some of the forest wildlife, including red squirrels.

Ham Hill Country Park, near Yeovil, Somerset

Unroll your rug on the grassy slopes and take in panoramic views of the Somerset Levels, Exmoor and the Mendip Hills as you munch your sarnies. The highest point is the site of an ancient hill fort and there are also wildflower meadows, woodland areas and a stone circle to explore.

Scotch eggs

A picnic staple for years, these delicious savoury parcels have been enjoying a well-deserved comeback in recent times

9 medium eggs
500g pork sausagemeat
1 tsp chopped fresh thyme
¼ tsp cayenne pepper
250g plain flour
50ml semi-skimmed milk
150g dried breadcrumbs
Sunflower oil, for deep-frying

Makes 8
Prep time: 20 mins,
plus chilling time
Cook time: 30 mins

Per Scotch egg
445 cals, 22.4g fat, 7.4g sat fat,
1.6g total sugars, 1.2g salt

1 Place 8 eggs in a large pan and add enough cold water just to cover them. Bring to a simmer and cook for 6 minutes for a medium-set yolk. Remove from the pan and plunge into a large bowl of iced water to cool.

2 Meanwhile, place the sausagemeat in a bowl. Add the thyme, cayenne pepper and 2 tbsp cold water, and mix well. Using wet hands, shape into 8 patties, then chill in the fridge for 15 minutes.

3 Preheat the oven to 190ºC, fan 170ºC, gas 5. Shell the eggs. Flatten each sausagemeat patty into a circle and place an egg in the centre. Carefully wrap the sausagemeat around the egg, pressing the edges gently together.

4 Tip the flour into a small bowl. Break the remaining 1 egg into another bowl, add the milk and beat together. Tip the breadcrumbs into a third bowl.

5 Roll each egg in flour, then dip in the egg mixture and, finally, coat in the breadcrumbs.

6 Take a deep fat fryer or deep saucepan and pour in enough oil just to cover the eggs. Heat to 190ºC, at which temperature a cube of bread will sizzle and crisp up within 30 seconds of being dropped into the oil. Fry the Scotch eggs 2 at a time, for 2 minutes, until golden. Remove with a slotted spoon and place on a baking tray.

7 Cook the eggs in the oven for 10 minutes. Serve warm or cold.

Try this...
Great served with peppery watercress and a herby mayonnaise

Golden eggs

While the origins of the Scotch egg are unclear, they don't seem to have anything to do with Scotland! Fortnum & Mason (pictured), in London, claims to have invented them for rich coach travellers in 1738, but they may have evolved from an Indian dish made from minced meat and a boiled egg. Then again, they may have been a working man's portable lunch. Scotch eggs have long been a staple at traditional pubs and now gastropubs are in on the act, too.

Ultimate ploughman's picnic sandwich

A ploughman's lunch is one of the tastiest ways to enjoy a good chunk of mature Cheddar, and this all-in-one sarnie makes it easy to take along on your picnic

Good pub-licity

If the mere thought of ploughman's lunch has you conjuring up images of long-lost pastoral idylls, think again. The phrase ploughboy's lunch dates back to 1837, but the hearty snack of cheese, bread and pickle didn't really take off until the 1960s, when the Milk Marketing Board revived it – renaming it ploughman's lunch – as a tactic to sell British cheese in pubs. No matter.

The simple pairing of good, mature Cheddar and crusty bread, enhanced by the tang of chutney and pickles, gives this British pub classic an enduring appeal. A ploughman's is perfect served with a glass of beer, and the custom of teaming bread, cheese and ale goes back centuries – there's even mention of it being offered to bell-ringers at St Paul's in the 14th century. Ding dong.

1 x 400g Sainsbury's crusty white baguette, cut into 4 pieces
20g unsalted butter, softened
100g Taste the Difference apple & pear chutney
200g Taste the Difference West Country farmhouse mature Cheddar, thickly sliced
120g pickled onions, roughly chopped
2 small apples, to serve

1 Slice each piece of bread in half lengthways. Spread the bottom halves with butter and the top halves with chutney.

2 Place the Cheddar and pickled onion inside the bread. Wrap in foil or baking parchment to take to your picnic. Once there, slice the apples, place half in the baguettes and serve with the remaining slices.

Serves 4
Prep time: 10 mins

Per sandwich
607 cals, 23.5g fat, 14g sat fat, 17.7g total sugars, 3g salt

Bacon, cheese & chive tart

This mouthwatering tart is perfect picnic fare – just pick up a slice and tuck in. It's also delicious eaten warm as a simple supper

200g plain flour, plus extra
for dusting
100g unsalted butter, chilled
and cubed
Pinch of salt
1 egg yolk, beaten with 2 tbsp
chilled water
1 x 250g pack Sainsbury's
smoked bacon lardons
3 medium eggs, beaten
150ml half-fat crème fraîche
100ml semi-skimmed milk
100g extra mature Cheddar, grated
¼ x 25g pack Sainsbury's
fresh chives, chopped

Serves 8
**Prep time: 20 mins,
plus chilling time
Cook time: 1 hour**
....
Per serving
**386 cals, 26.8g fat, 14.3g sat
fat, 1.6g total sugars, 1.5g salt**

1 Place the flour, butter and salt in a food processor and pulse until the mixture resembles breadcrumbs. Tip into a bowl and add the egg yolk and water mixture, stirring until the pastry comes together. Shape into a large patty and wrap in clingfilm. Place in the fridge to chill for 30 minutes.

2 Preheat the oven to 190ºC, fan 170ºC, gas 5.

3 On a lightly floured surface, roll out the pastry to the thickness of a £1 coin and use it to line a 23cm loose-bottomed tart tin, 3cm deep, leaving any excess overhanging. Prick the base with a fork and place in the fridge to chill for 15 minutes.

4 Line the pastry case with baking parchment and top with baking beans or uncooked rice. Bake blind in the oven for 15 minutes, then remove the beans or rice and the parchment, and bake the pastry for a further 10–12 minutes, until golden. Remove from the oven and cool for a few minutes, then trim the excess pastry using a sharp knife. Reduce the oven temperature to 180ºC, fan 160ºC, gas 4.

5 Meanwhile, fry the lardons in a non-stick frying pan for 5–10 minutes, until crispy. In a large bowl, lightly whisk the eggs with the crème fraîche, milk, half the Cheddar and half the chives.

6 Scatter the fried lardons into the pastry case, pour in the egg mixture, then sprinkle over the remaining cheese and chives.

7 Bake in the oven for 30–35 minutes, until just set and golden. Remove and leave to cool. Great served with a salad.

Making your own mayonnaise is much easier than you think

Top tip...
If the mayo splits, whisk in 1 egg yolk mixed with 1 tbsp just-boiled water

Potato salad

Gherkins and capers add extra bite to this potato salad, which is especially tasty with homemade mayonnaise

750g new potatoes, halved if large
2 gherkins, finely chopped
1½ tbsp capers, drained
2 tbsp finely chopped fresh flat-leaf parsley
½ bunch spring onions, sliced

For the mayonnaise
2 large egg yolks, at room temperature
1 heaped tsp English mustard powder
½ tbsp white wine vinegar

250ml sunflower or groundnut oil

Serves 4
Prep time: 20 mins
Cook time: 15 mins

Per serving
457 cals, **33.8g fat,
7g sat fat, 3.4g total
sugars, 0.7g salt**

1 Place the potatoes in a pan of cold water. Bring to the boil, then simmer for 12–15 minutes, until tender. Drain and allow to cool.

2 Meanwhile, make the mayonnaise. Place the egg yolks, mustard powder and vinegar in a food processor and blend. While the motor is running, drizzle the oil very slowly through the lid, incorporating each drop before adding more. Continue adding the oil until the mayonnaise reaches the desired consistency, adding a little warm water if it becomes too thick. Add more mustard powder or vinegar to taste and season with salt and white pepper.

3 Tip the potatoes into a large bowl and mix in half the mayonnaise, setting the rest aside to make the coleslaw (see right). Mix in the gherkins, capers, parsley and most of the spring onions and season to taste with salt and freshly ground black pepper. Serve sprinkled with the remaining spring onions.

Cook's note: this recipe contains raw eggs. Keep the mayonnaise in a sterilised container in the fridge for up to 3 days

Coleslaw

Finely shred 225g white cabbage into a large bowl. Add 2 large carrots, peeled and grated, and 1 finely chopped onion. Stir through half the homemade mayonnaise (see left), or use 125ml shop-bought mayo if you're short of time. Mix together well and serve. For a variation, add a handful of raisins and walnuts, or sprinkle with poppy seeds.

Serves 4
Prep time: 20 mins

Per serving 372 cals, 33.6g fat, 6.9g sat fat, 10.3g total sugars, 0.1g salt

Try this...

Stir through 2 x 185g tins tuna, drained, to turn this into a light supper

A new leaf

The word 'sallet' first appeared in English in the 14th century and referred to green leaves, sometimes served with flowers. The 'grand sallet' arrived in the 17th century, with any number of ingredients, including fruit. In 1699, John Evelyn devoted an entire book, *Acetaria*, to salads, and by the 19th century, Brits were taking their salads quite seriously. Today, we enjoy countless variations with influences from far and wide.

Big British salad

Vibrant and tasty, this crowd-pleaser is made with some of the country's finest home-grown fresh ingredients

500g baby new potatoes, halved if large
200g fine asparagus
½ tbsp white wine vinegar
1 tbsp lemon juice
½ tsp caster sugar
3 tbsp sunflower oil
½ tsp English mustard powder
1 red onion, finely sliced
⅓ cucumber, sliced and halved
100g radishes, quartered
2 tbsp roughly chopped fresh flat-leaf parsley
1 x 75g bag Sainsbury's watercress

Serves 6
Prep time: 15 mins, plus cooling time
Cook time: 15 mins

Per serving
133 cals, 6.2g fat, 0.8g sat fat, 3.8g total sugars, trace salt

1 Place the potatoes in a pan of cold water. Bring to the boil, then simmer for 12–15 minutes, until tender. Drain and allow to cool. Meanwhile, place the asparagus in a pan of boiling water and simmer for 1½ minutes, then drain and refresh in cold water.

2 Place the vinegar, lemon juice, sugar, oil and mustard powder in a jug. Season with salt and freshly ground black pepper, whisk together, then set aside or store in an airtight container to take on your picnic.

3 Place the onion, cucumber, radishes and parsley in a large bowl, add the potatoes and asparagus, then fold through the watercress. To serve, add the dressing and toss gently until coated.

Savoury muffins

Preheat the oven to 200°C, fan 180°C, gas 6. Heat 1 tbsp olive oil in a pan. Sauté 1 sliced red onion for 5 minutes, until soft, then set aside. In a bowl, mix together 250g sifted plain flour, 1 tbsp baking powder and a pinch of salt. In a jug, beat 2 large eggs with 200ml semi-skimmed milk, then gently fold into the flour. Stir in the onion, 50g goats' cheese, crumbled into small chunks, and 4 finely chopped sprigs of rosemary. Do not over-mix. Line a 12-hole muffin tin with squares of baking parchment, spoon in the mixture and sprinkle with rosemary leaves. Bake for 20 minutes.

Makes 12
Prep time: 15 mins Cook time: 25 mins

Per muffin 127 cals, 3.7g fat, 1.4g sat fat, 1.9g total sugars, 0.5g salt

Top tip...

To avoid melting, pack the tiffin in a cool-bag with a few bottles of chilled water

Chocolate tiffin

This easy-peasy refrigerator cake is the ideal sweet treat to round off your picnic

100g shelled pistachios
150g unsalted butter, plus extra for greasing
2 tbsp golden syrup
1 x 200g bar Sainsbury's smooth dark chocolate
150g digestive biscuits
100g raisins
50g dried cranberries

Makes 16 squares
Prep time: 10 mins,
plus setting time
Cook time: 15 mins

Per serving
242 cals, **16.9g** fat,
9g sat fat, **14.1g** total
sugars, **0.2g** salt

1 Lightly grease a 20cm square tin and line with clingfilm. Preheat the oven to 160°C, fan 140°C, gas 3. Place the pistachios on a baking tray and roast in the oven for about 10 minutes – watch carefully to make sure they don't burn. Remove and roughly chop.

2 Meanwhile, over a low heat, melt the butter, syrup and chocolate in a medium pan, stirring continuously.

3 Place the biscuits in a large, sealable plastic bag and crush with a rolling pin, leaving some larger pieces. Tip into the melted chocolate mixture, along with the roasted pistachios, raisins and cranberries, and stir until well combined.

4 Spoon into the prepared tin and place in the fridge for at least 4 hours, until set. Allow the tiffin to reach room temperature before slicing into squares, then serve.

I should cocoa

Chocolate was first sold in England in the 1650s, when it was advertised as a drink that 'cures and preserves the body of many diseases'. Chocolate houses soon sprang up all over London and became fashionable meeting places – the Garrick Club started life as the Cocoa-Tree Chocolate House. Bitter and coarse by today's standards, the first chocolate bar appeared in 1847. It wasn't until 1875 that a Swiss manufacturer had the bright idea of adding milk – first powdered and later condensed – for a superior taste and texture. During World War I, chocolate was even included in soldiers' rations, providing a welcome taste of home.

Find the right recipe at a glance

Halloumi kebabs

Eton mess

Ultimate ploughman's picnic sandwich

Roast rib of beef

1 of your 5 a day

Pavlova

Big British salad

2 of your 5 a day

Cawl

3 of your 5 a day

Chilli con carne **47**

Starters and soups

Cock-a-leekie soup **209**
Cullen skink **202**
London particular **129**
Potted crab **101**
Scotch broth **199**
Smoked trout pâté (with pickled cucumber) **105**
Watercress soup **125**

Side dishes

Brussels sprouts with pancetta
& hazelnuts **237**
Champ **189**
Coleslaw **293**
Maple-glazed carrots
& parsnips **237**
Neeps 'n' tatties **201**
Potato farls **189**
Potato salad **293**
Roast potatoes **237**
Yorkshire puddings **69**

Champ

Mains

Anglesey eggs **173**
Beef & stout pie **186**
Cawl **165**
Chicken tikka masala **39**
Chilli con carne **47**
Fish & chips (with mushy peas) **14**
Fish pie **17**
Game pie **204**
Haggis with neeps 'n' tatties **201**
Honeyed Welsh lamb **168**

Lancashire hotpot **72**
Norfolk dumplings
(with savoury mince) **114**
Norfolk plough pudding **113**
Poacher's pie **106**
Roast pork loin **110**
Roast rib of beef **18**
Roast turkey **234**
Sausages & mash
(with onion gravy) **22**
Scallop & mushroom pie **182**
Scotch broth **199**
Scouse **63**
Shepherd's pie **21**
Shropshire fidget pie **84**
Somerset chicken in cider **145**
Spaghetti bolognese **42**
Steak & kidney pudding **24**
Suffolk cyder mussels **102**
Sweet & sour chicken **40**
Thai green chicken curry **45**
Toad in the hole **27**

Fish & chips

Game pie

Desserts

Apple pie **31**
Bakewell tart **88**
Bread & butter pudding **33**
Cambridge burnt cream **117**
Cheesecake **55**
Chocolate mousse **53**
Christmas pudding **238**
Cranachan **215**
Eton mess **130**
Gypsy tart **135**
Jam roly-poly (with homemade custard) **34**
Lincolnshire steamed carrot pudding **94**
Malvern pudding **93**
Nottingham apple batter pudding **87**
Pancakes **225**

Bakewell tart

Traditional lemonade

Macaroons

Victoria sandwich

Simnel cake

Index

Conversion table

Weights		Volume		Measurements		Oven temperatures		fan	gas
15g	½ oz	25ml	1fl oz	2mm	1/16 in	110°C	90°C		
25g	1 oz	50ml	2fl oz	3mm	1/8 in	120°C	100°C		½
40g	1½ oz	75ml	3fl oz	4mm	1/6 in	140°C	120°C		1
50g	2 oz	100ml	4fl oz	5mm	¼ in	150°C	130°C		2
60g	2½ oz	150ml	5fl oz (¼ pint)	1cm	½ in	160°C	140°C		3
75g	3 oz	175ml	6fl oz	2cm	¾ in	180°C	160°C		4
100g	3½ oz	200ml	7fl oz	2.5cm	1 in	190°C	170°C		5
125g	4 oz	225ml	8fl oz	3cm	1¼ in	200°C	180°C		6
150g	5 oz	250ml	9fl oz	4cm	1½ in	220°C	200°C		7
175g	6 oz	300ml	10fl oz (½ pint)	4.5cm	1¾ in	230°C	210°C		8
200g	7 oz	350ml	13fl oz	5cm	2 in	240°C	220°C		9
225g	8 oz	400ml	14fl oz	6cm	2½ in				
250g	9 oz	450ml	16fl oz (¾ pint)	7.5cm	3 in				
275g	10 oz	600ml	20fl oz (1 pint)	9cm	3½ in				
300g	11 oz	750ml	25fl oz (1¼ pints)	10cm	4 in				
350g	12 oz	900ml	30fl oz (1½ pints)	13cm	5 in				
375g	13 oz	1 litre	34fl oz (1¾ pints)	13.5cm	5¼ in				
400g	14 oz	1.2 litres	40fl oz (2 pints)	15cm	6 in				
425g	15 oz	1.5 litres	52fl oz (2½ pints)	16cm	6½ in				
450g	1lb	1.8 litres	60fl oz (3 pints)	18cm	7in				
500g	1lb 2 oz			19cm	7½ in				
650g	1lb 7 oz			20cm	8in				
675g	1½ lb			23cm	9in				
700g	1lb 9 oz			24cm	9½ in				
750g	1lb 11 oz			25.5cm	10 in				
900g	2lb			28cm	11 in				
1kg	2lb 4 oz			30cm	12 in				
1.5kg	3lb 6 oz			32.5cm	13 in				
				35cm	14 in				

Credits for photography and additional words
Page 30 Courtesy of the Bramley Apple Campaign, www.bramleyapples.co.uk
Page 72 Betty Driver photo: courtesy of ITV Granada Picture Archive
Page 170 John Masefield poetry: courtesy of The Society of Authors as the Literary Representative of the Estate of John Masefield
Page 186 Belfast photo: David Taylor
Pages 98 and 158 Scenic photos: Kathy De Whitt
Page 80 Supplier portrait: Jonathan Flint
Alamy, Bridgeman, Corbis, Getty Images, istock, Mary Evans, Sainsbury's Archive and Travel Pictures

Seven.

Credits

Editorial
Head of content Helen Renshaw
Editors Jo Clifton, Elaine Gowran
Sub editors and writers Beverley D'Silva, Jo Froude, Ward Hellewell, Lauren Hoffman, Sara Norman, Gill Wing

Food
Acting food editor Hannah Yeadon
Food stylists Valerie Barrett, Anna Burges-Lumsden, Sal Henley, Mima Sinclair
Food assistant Lottie Covell

Design
Senior art director David Jenkins
Design and style director Tim Mapleston
Design and art direction Nina Brennan
Stylist Morag Farquhar

Account management
Senior account director Lynne de Lacy
Account executive Alex Pearce
Publishing director Dorcas Jamieson

Photography
Michael Hart

For Sainsbury's
Book team Phil Carroll, Sharon Nightingale
Content team Sarah Ellis, Alex McDonald
Nutrition Annie Denny, Becky Williams
Product development/safety Nikki Mosley, Susi Richards
Supply chain Lee Scott, Natalie Sumner

Print & production
Production manager Mike Lamb
Colour origination F1 Colour Ltd
Printers Butler Tanner & Dennis Ltd, Frome and London

Special thanks to...
Patricia Baker, Angela Ellis, Frances Ewings, Claire Frankland, Phil Mundy, Sarah Peak, Howard Shooter, Tania Smith, Jayne Stewart

Step back in time

Located in the Museum of Docklands, the Sainsbury's Archive is a unique collection of more than 16,000 documents, photographs and objects which illustrate the history of today's supermarket chain. It also shows how shopping and eating habits in the UK have changed since the first Sainsbury's shop opened in 1869. For more information, visit museumindocklands.org.uk/sainsburyarchive.

Seven.

FSC
www.fsc.org
MIX
Paper from responsible sources
FSC® C023561

GREAT BRITISH BOOKS
PUBLISHED & PRINTED IN THE UK